I0833214

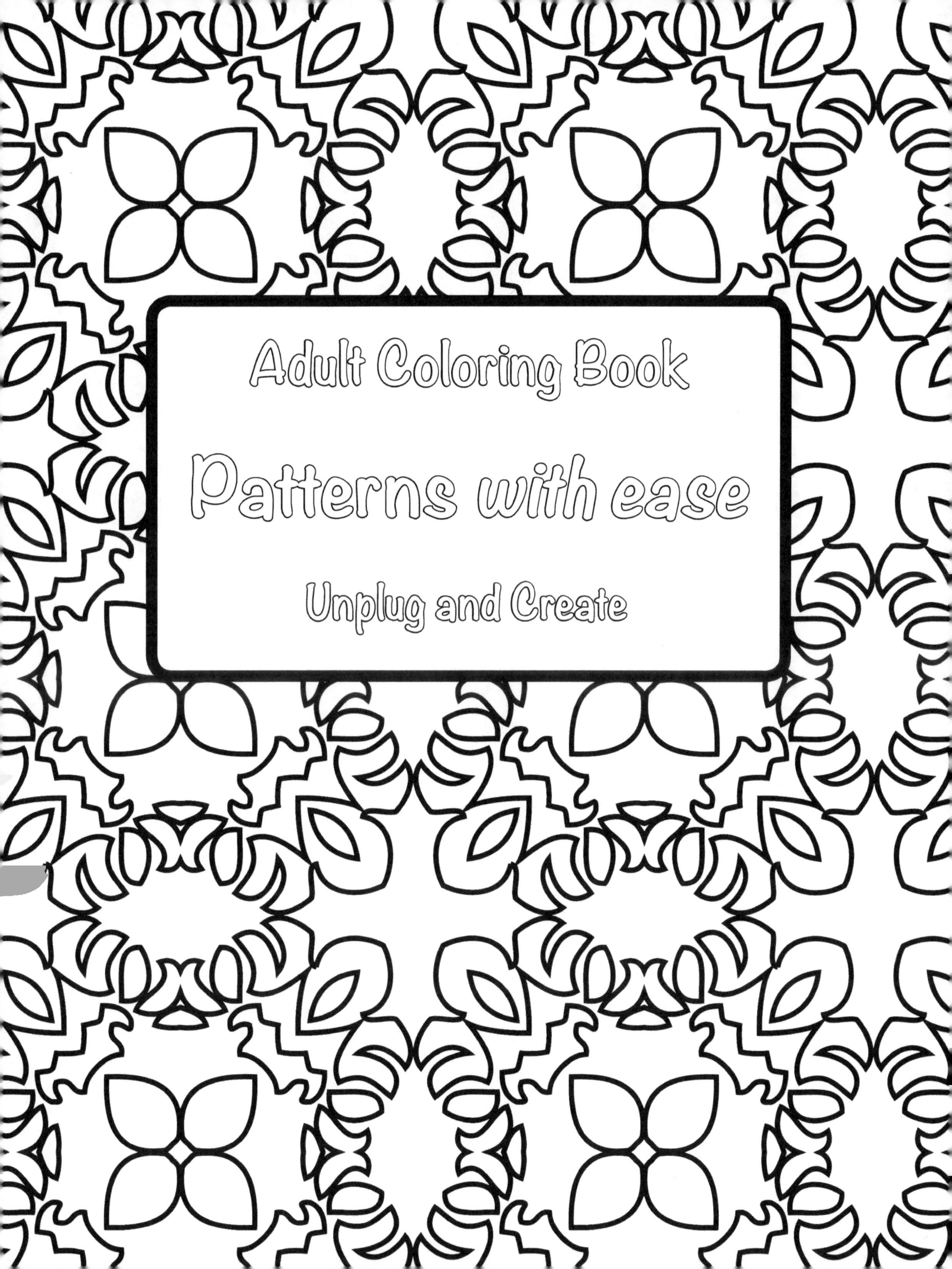
Adult Coloring Book
Patterns with ease
Unplug and Create

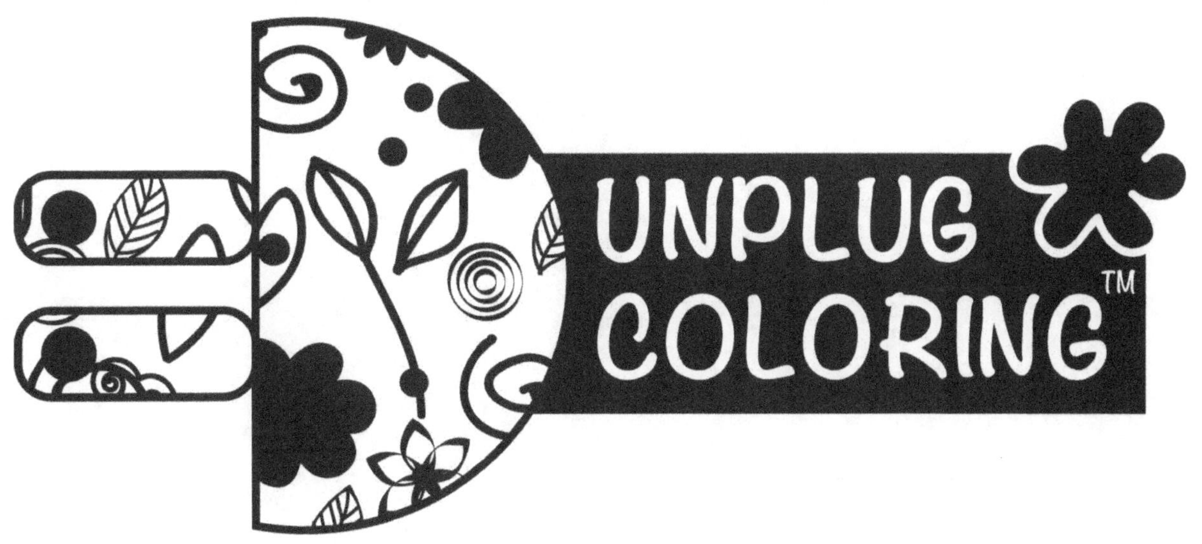

Visit unplugcoloring.com
for free coloring sheets,
new product releases and keep

CONNECTED

to us!

Published by Unplug Coloring
Fishers, IN 46037
www.unplugcoloring.com
sales@unplugcoloring.com

Design and production: Unplug Coloring

ISBN: 978-0-9974900-3-9
Made in the USA

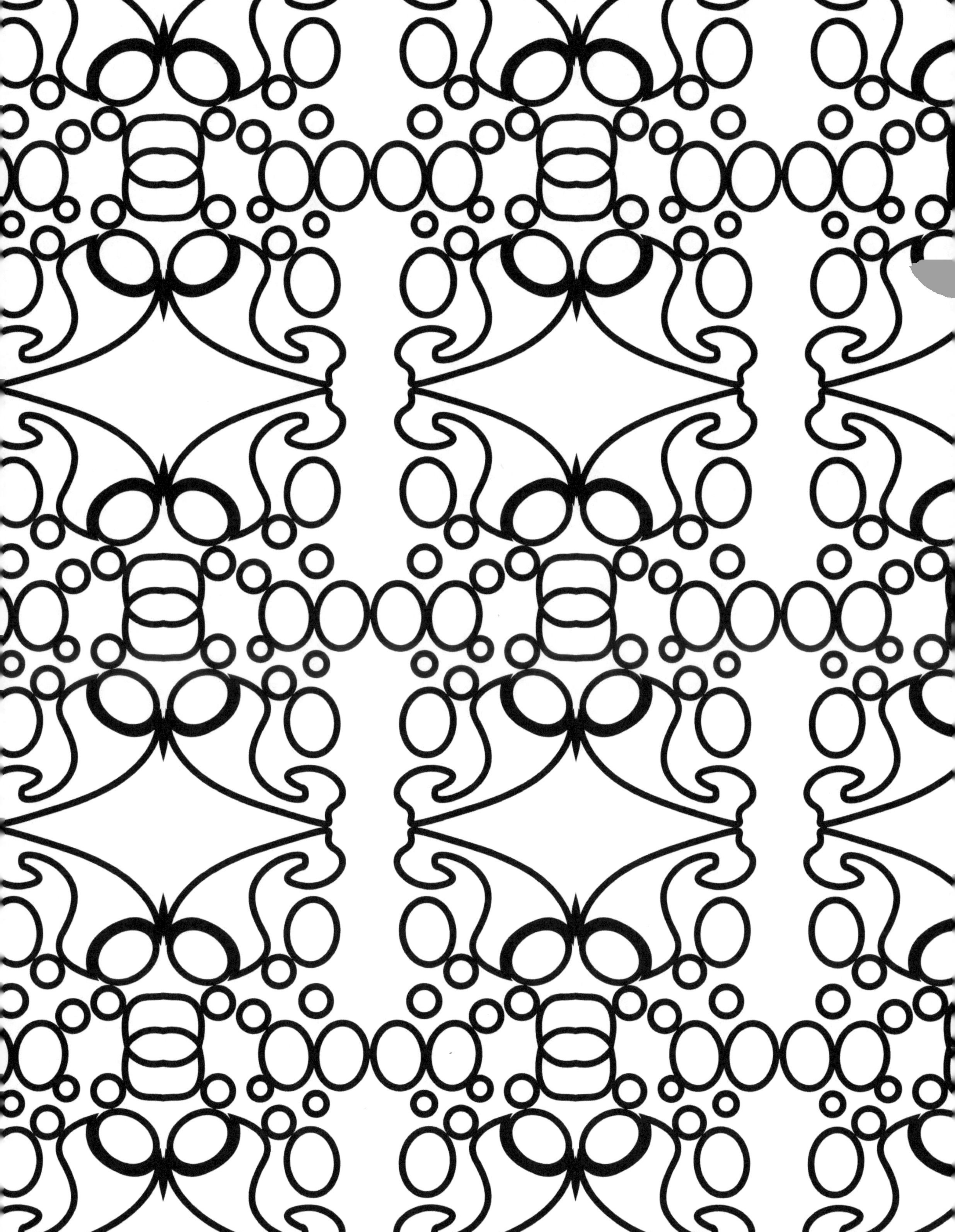

Sketch, Doodle & Blot!

These pages are provided to act as blotters to protect your art.

Be Creative!
Use these pages to sketch or doodle.

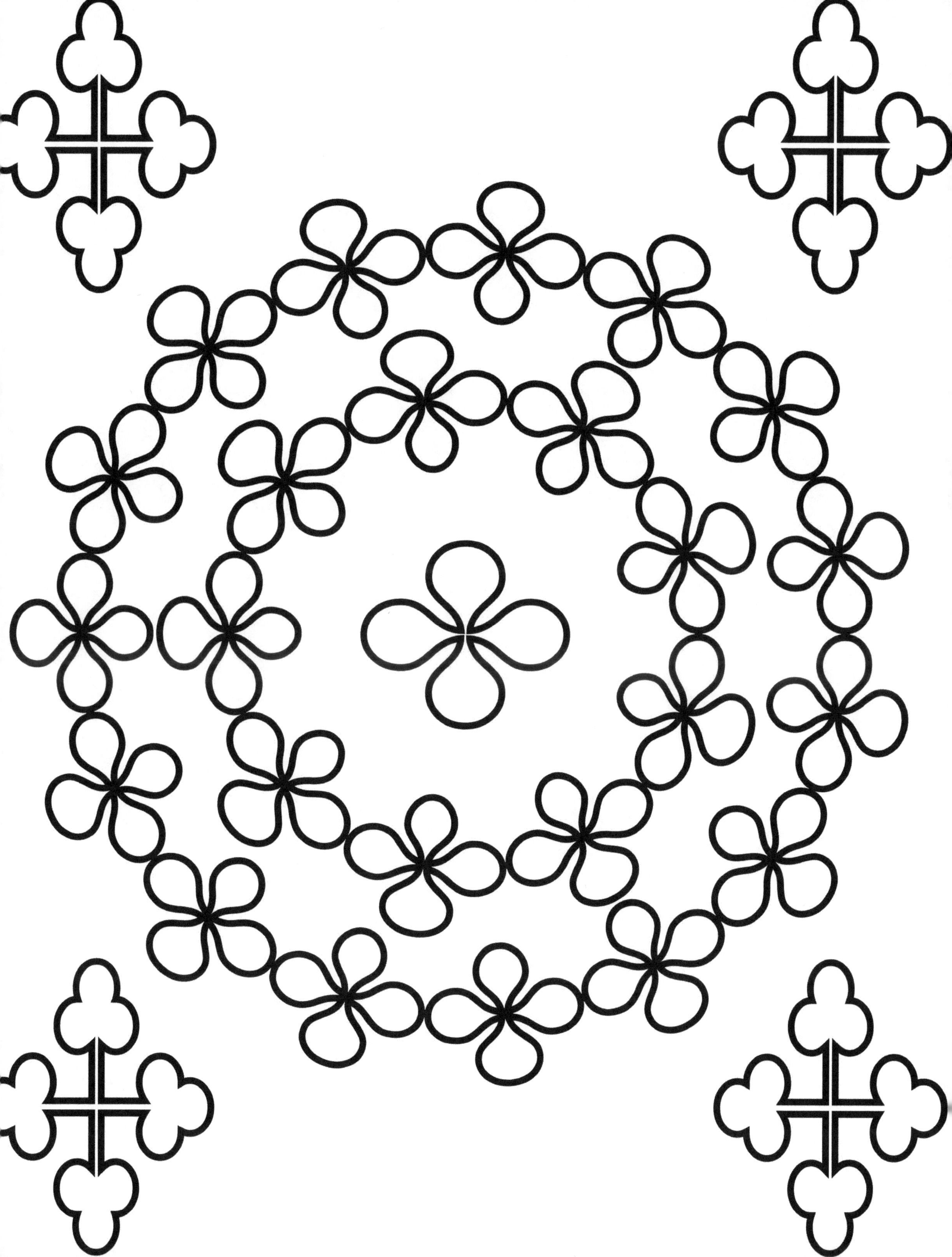

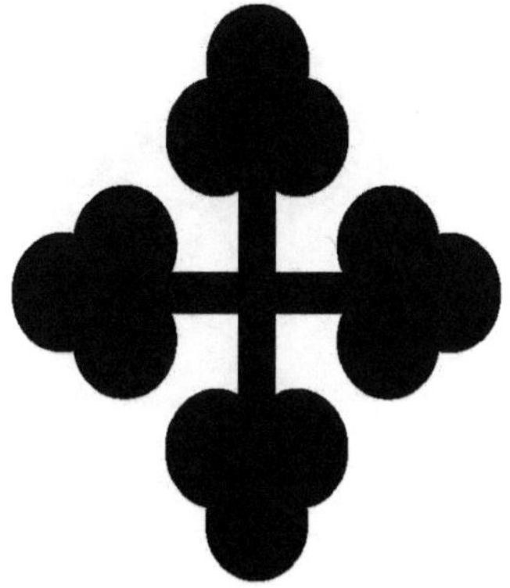

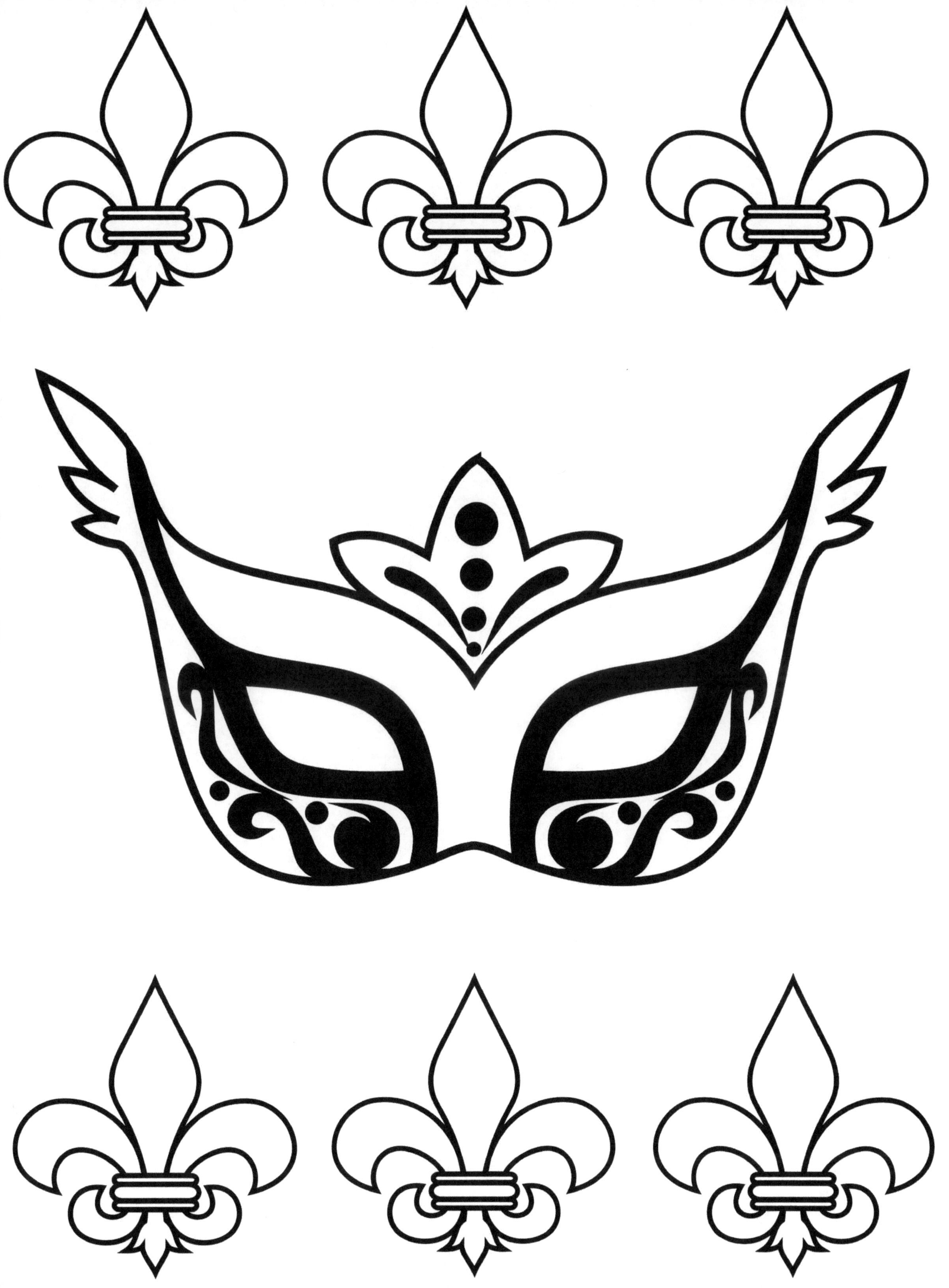

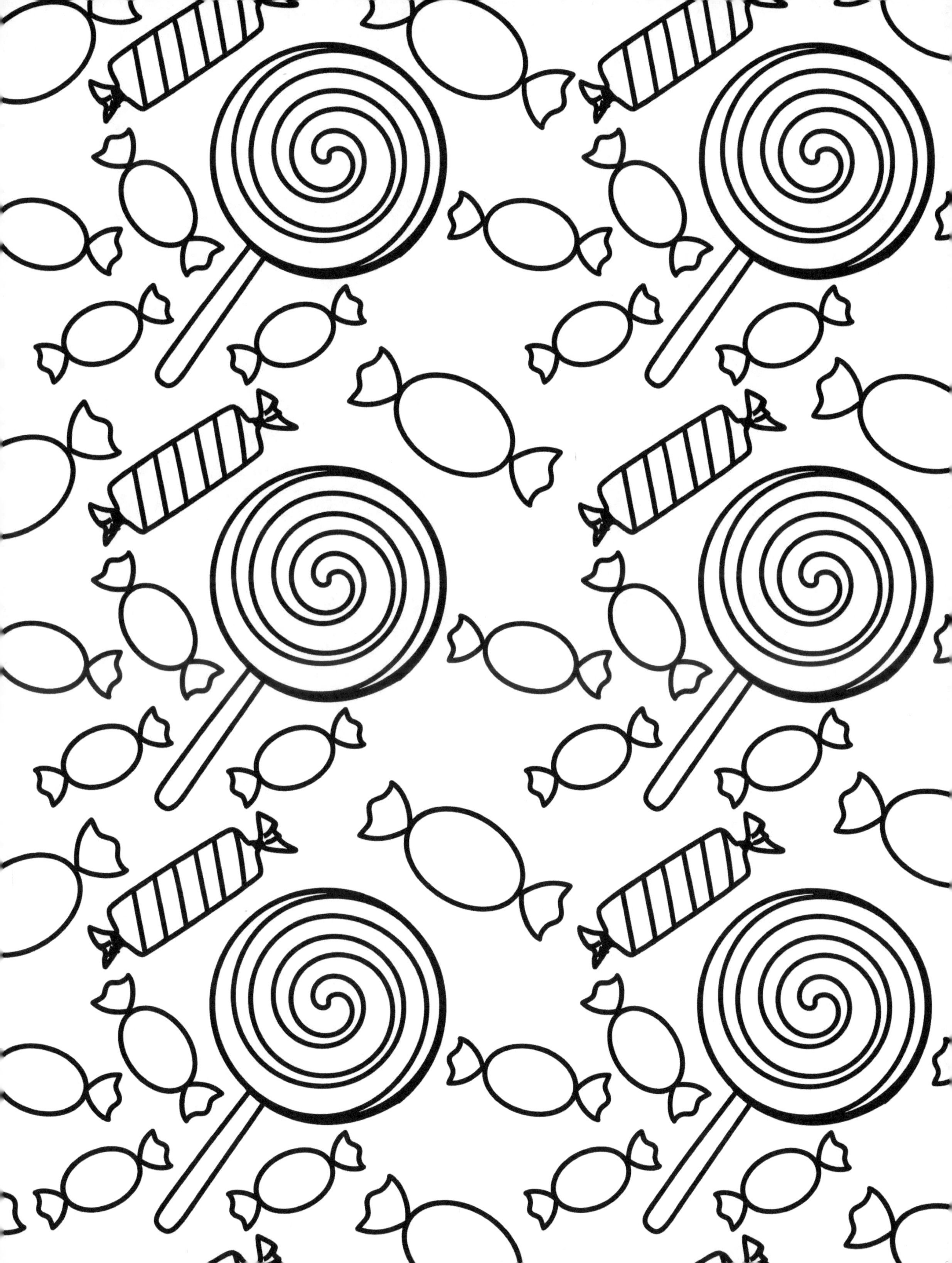

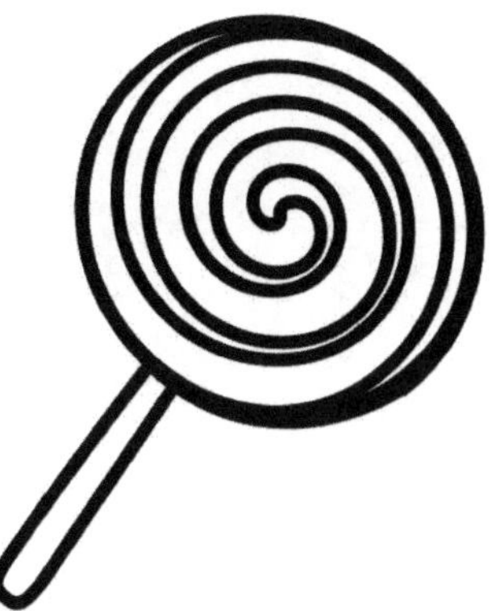

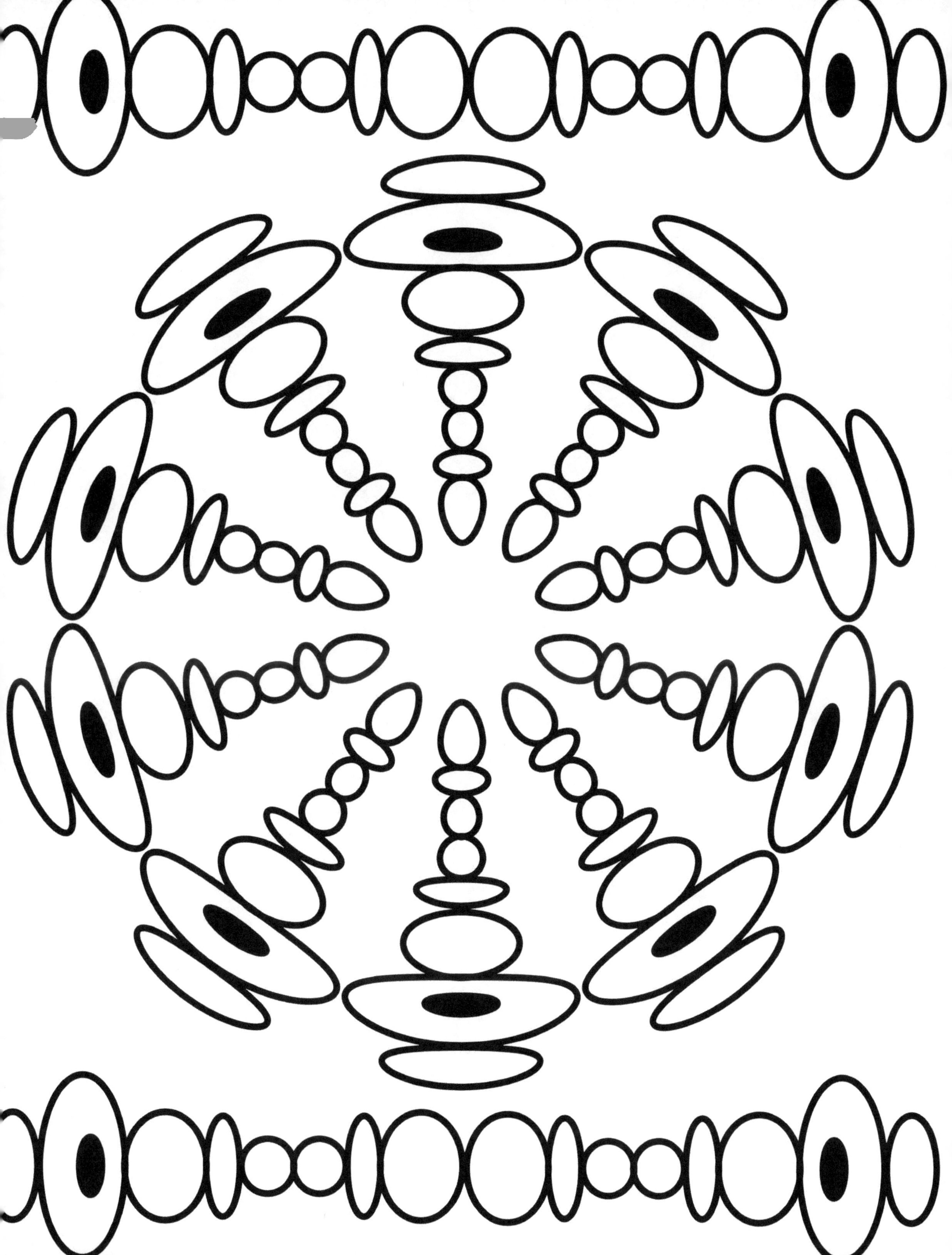

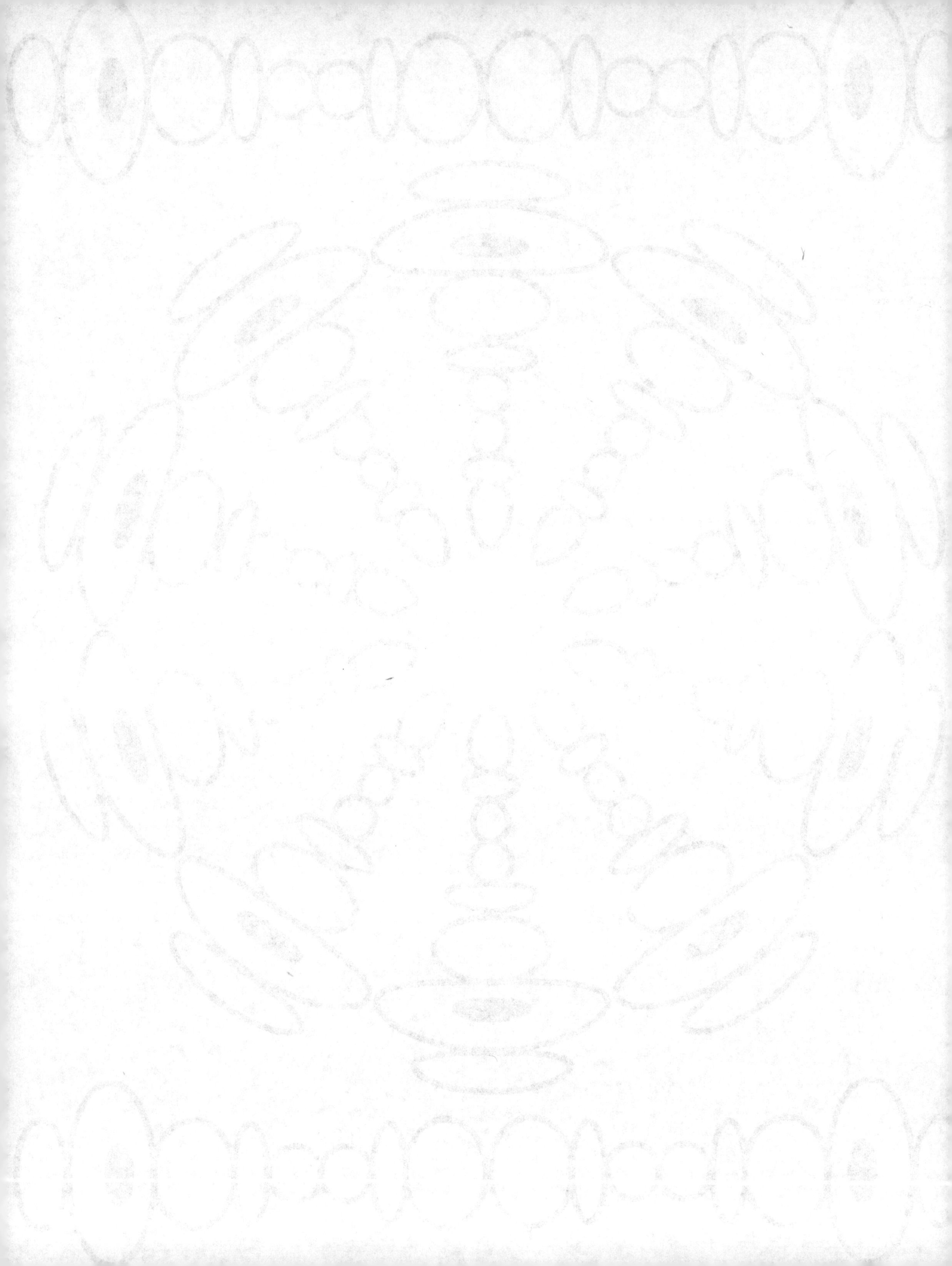

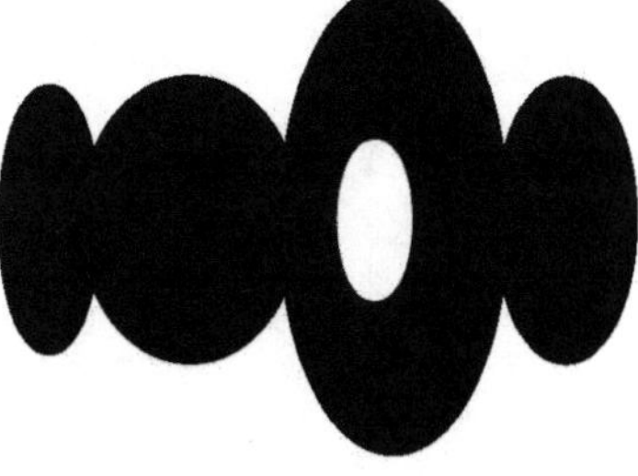

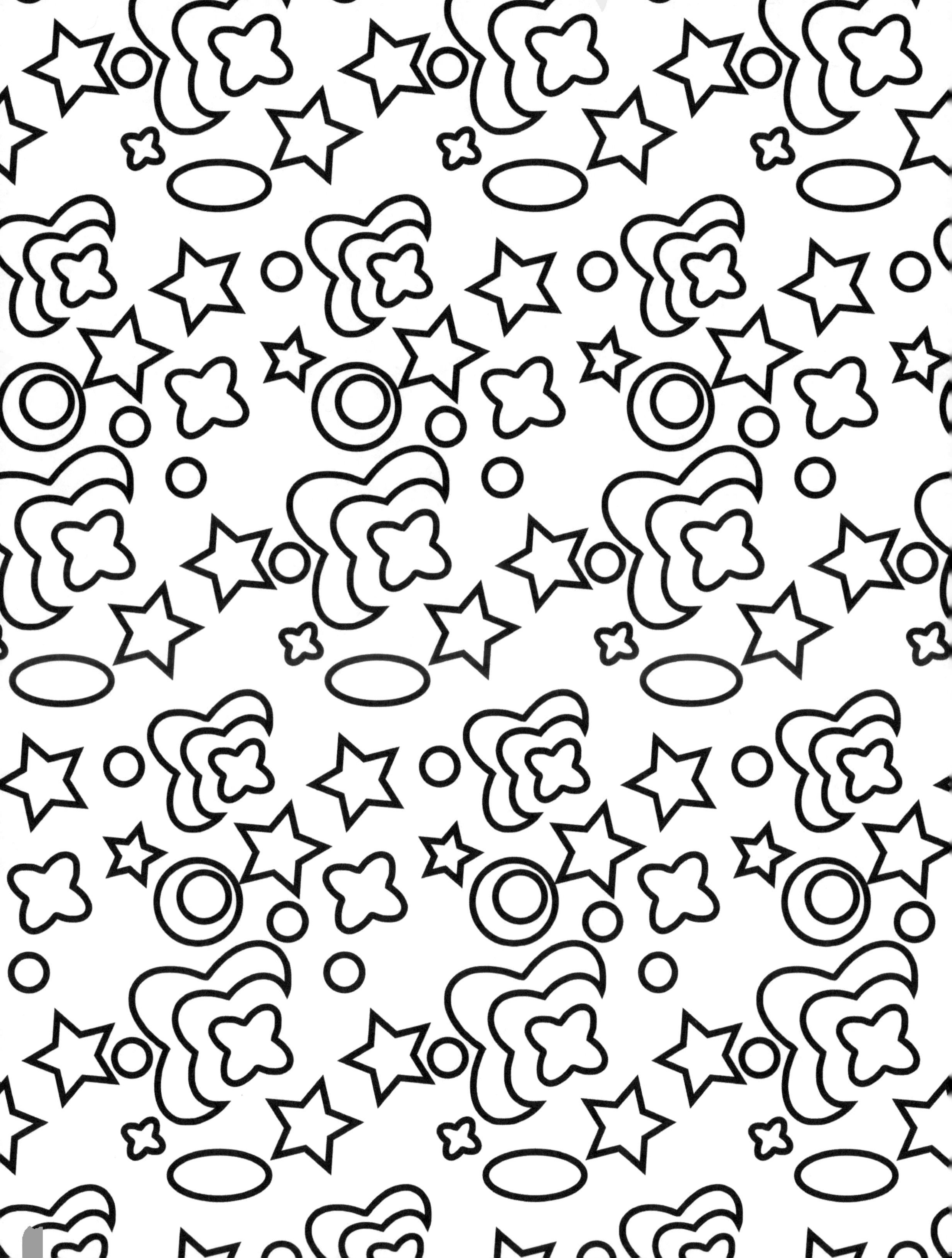

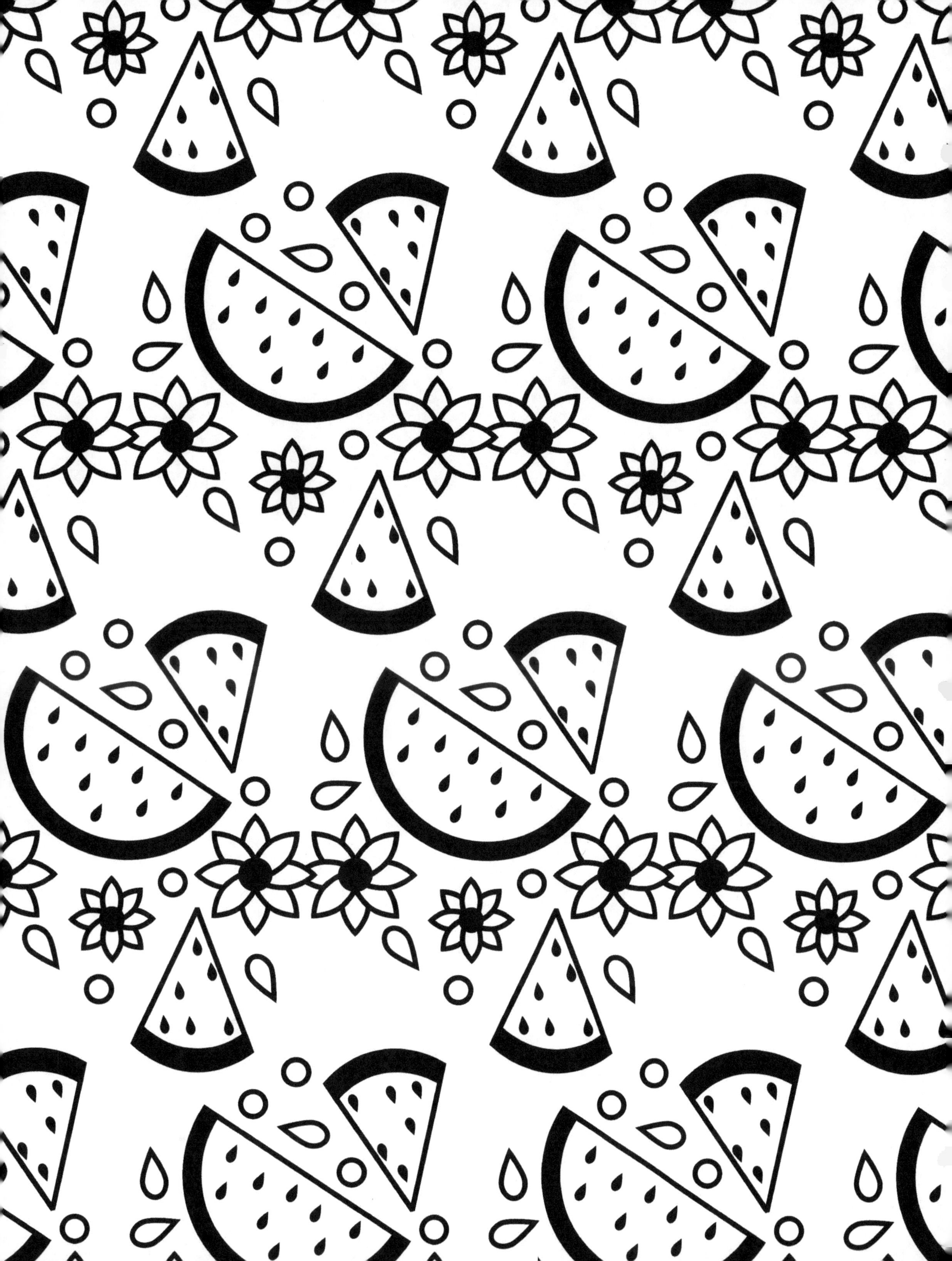

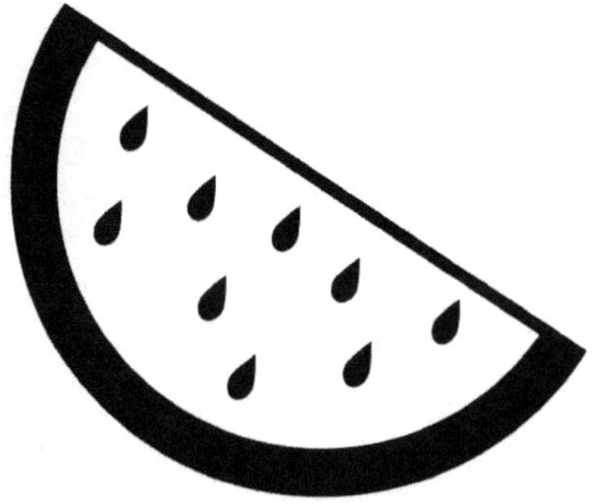

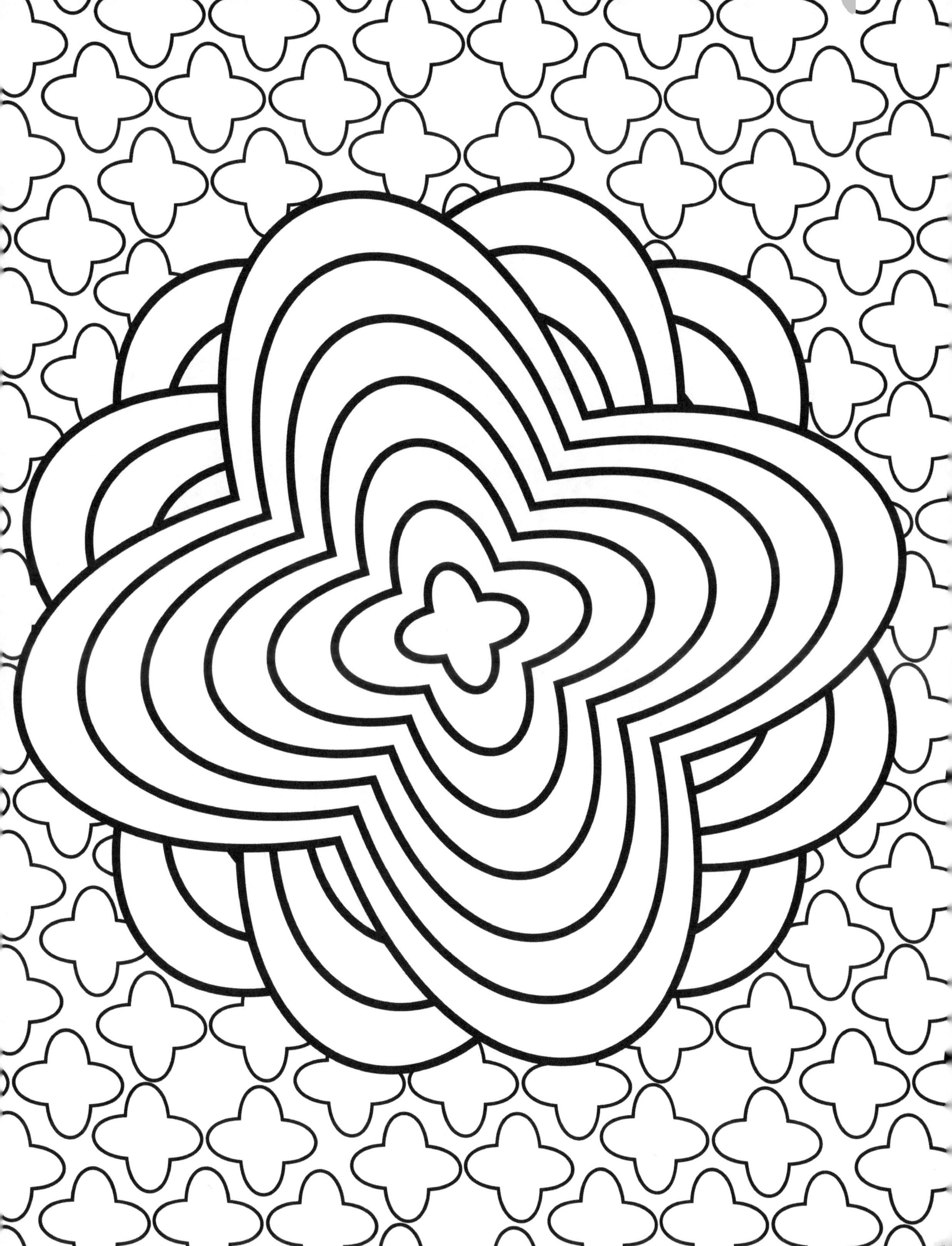

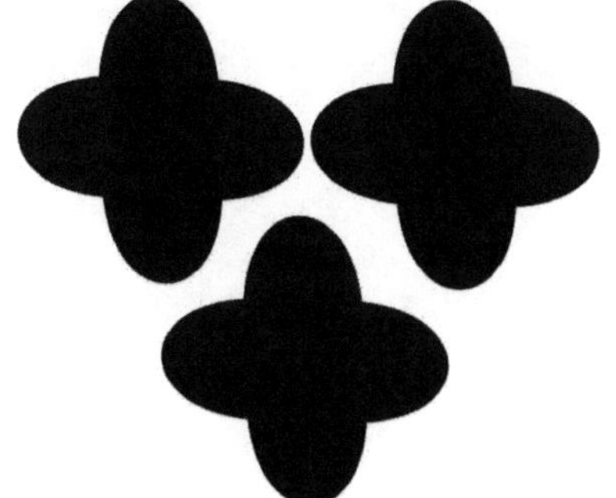

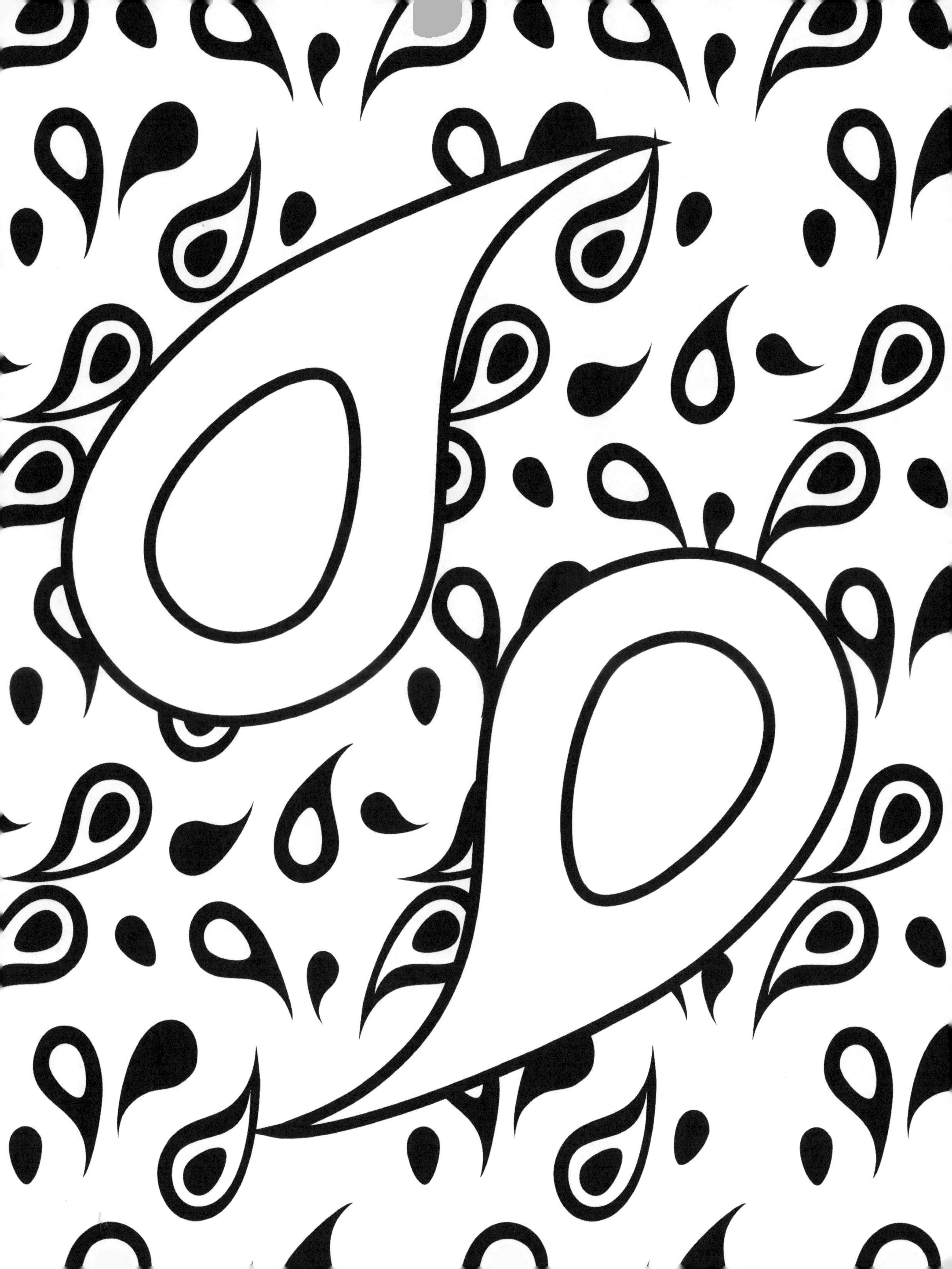

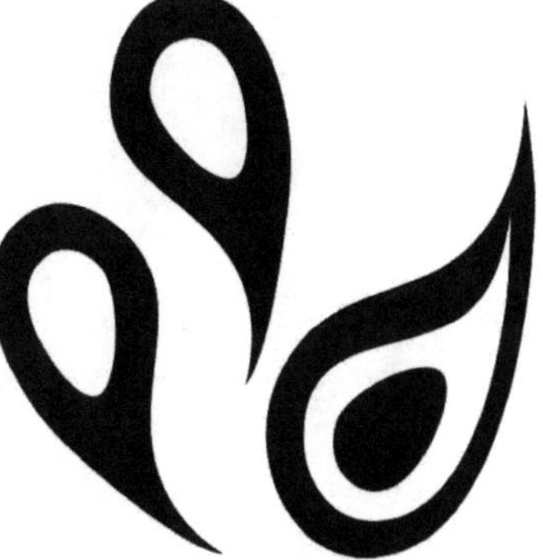

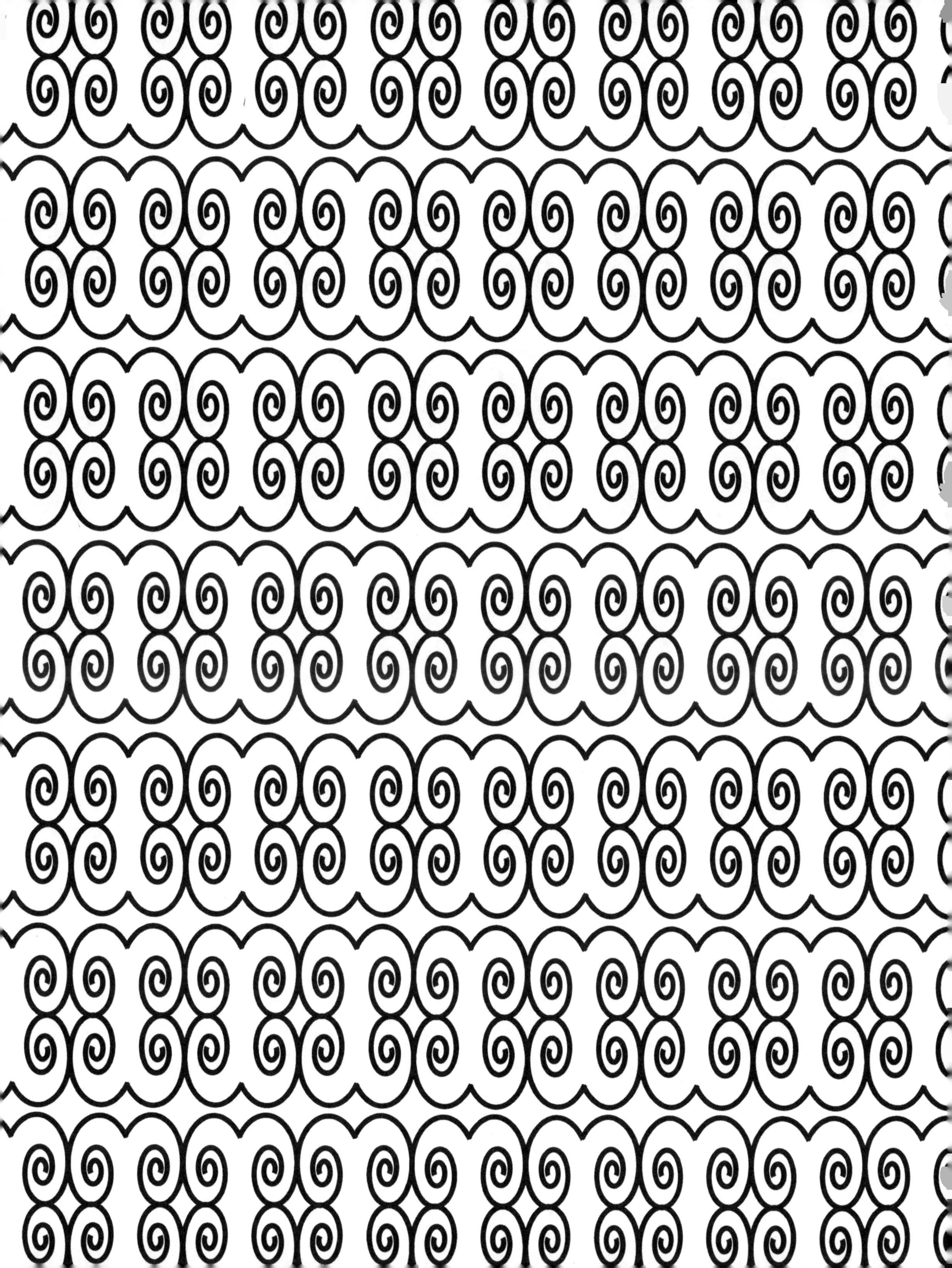

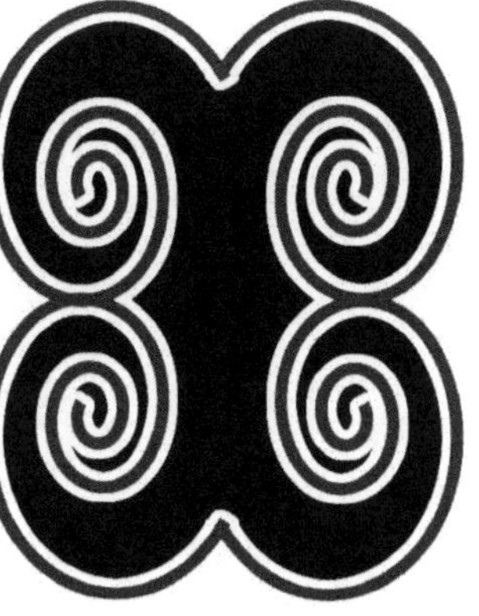

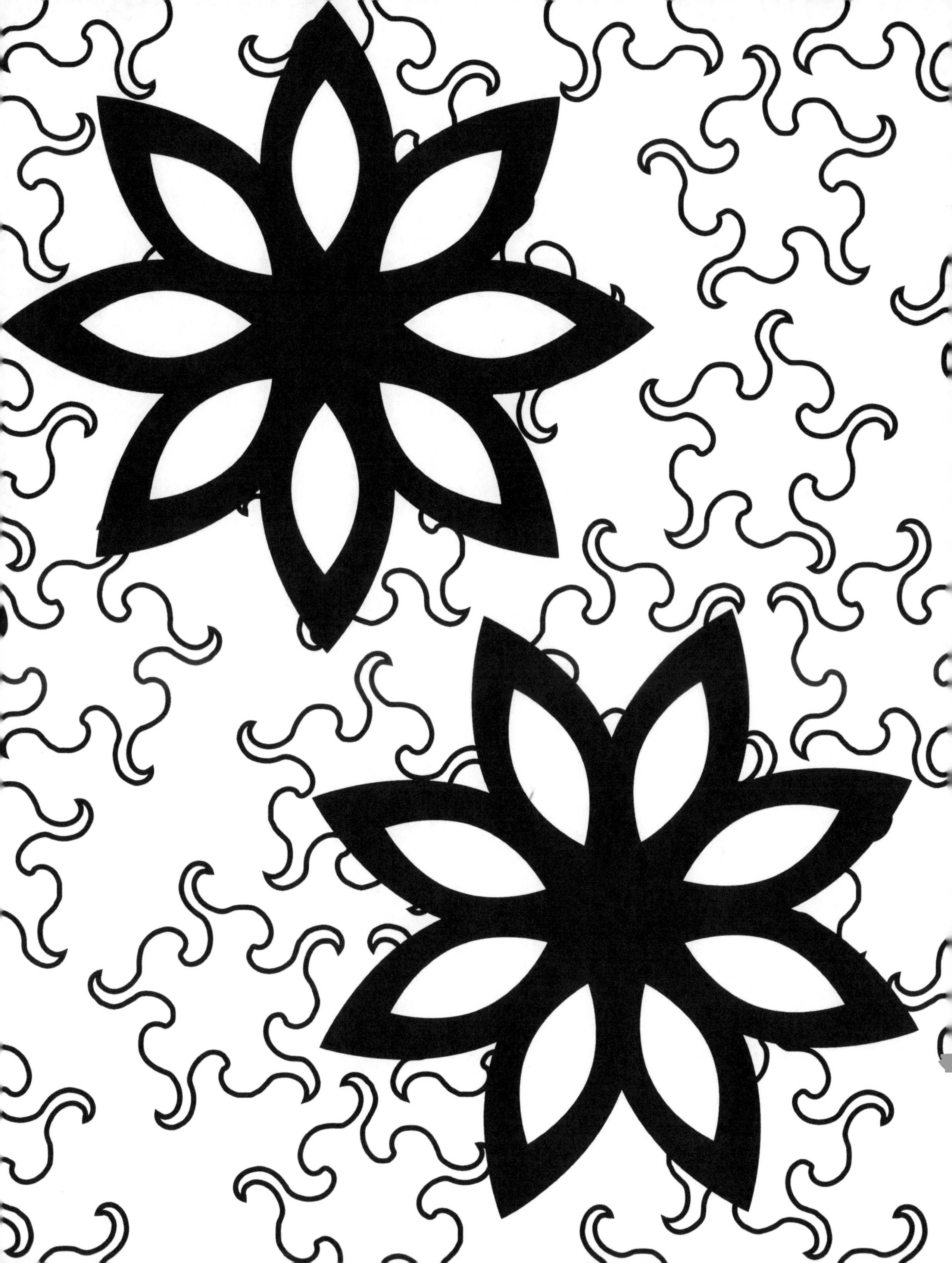

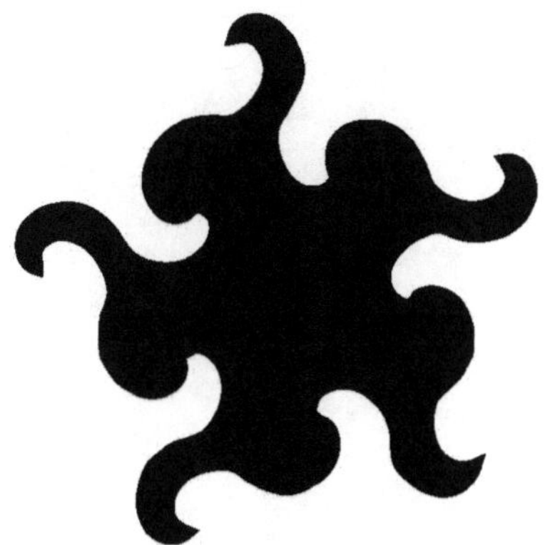

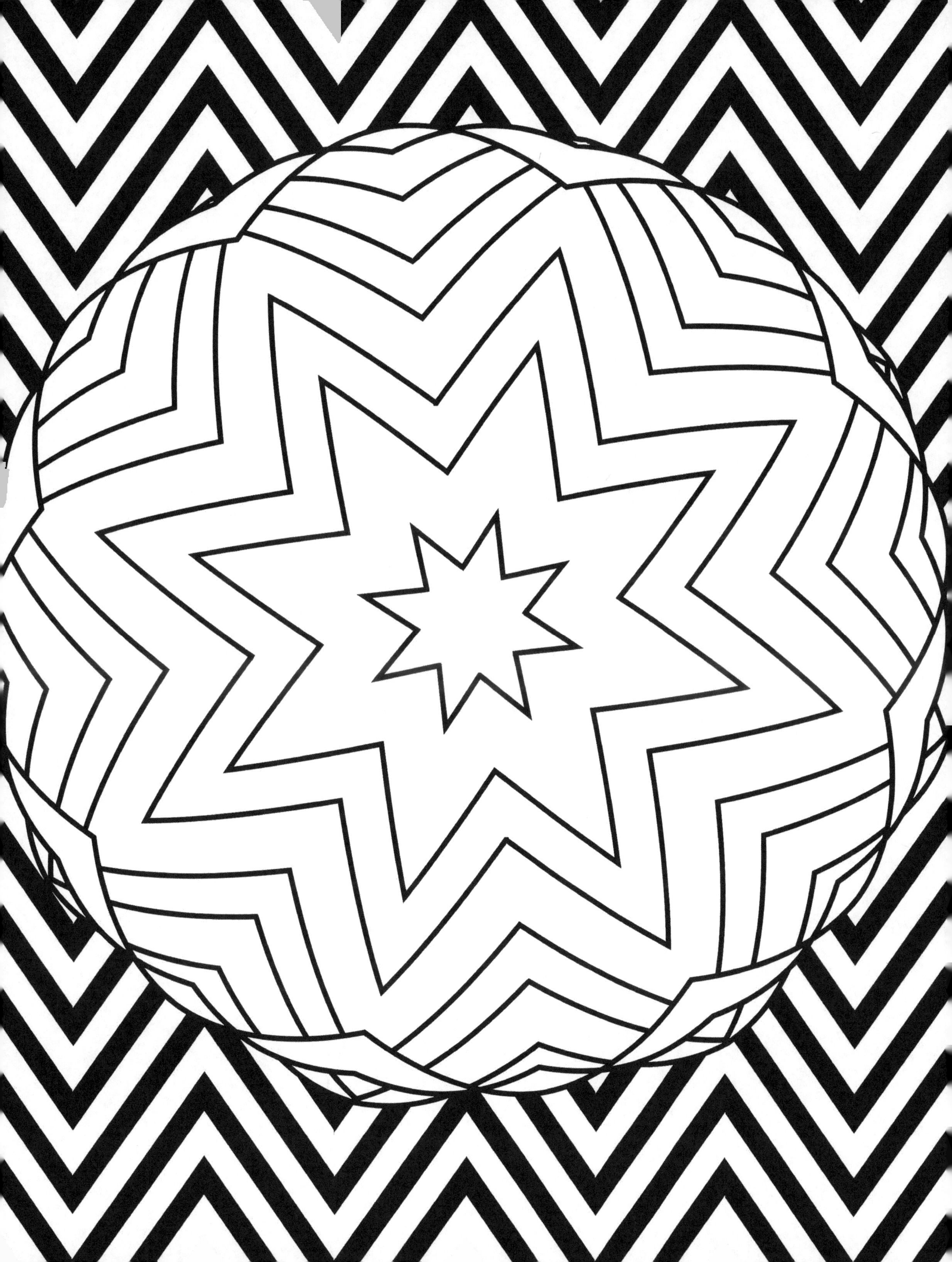

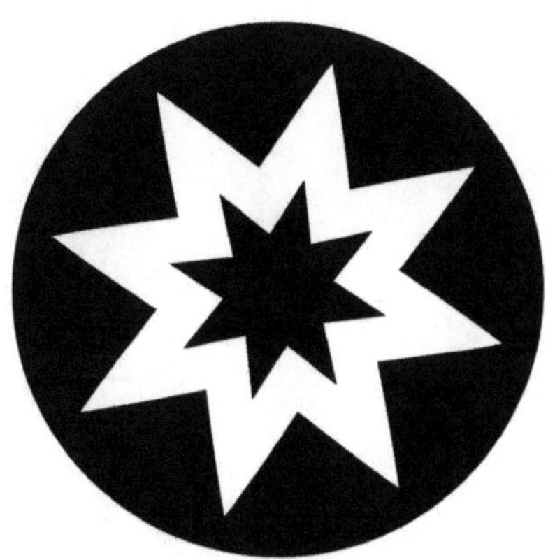

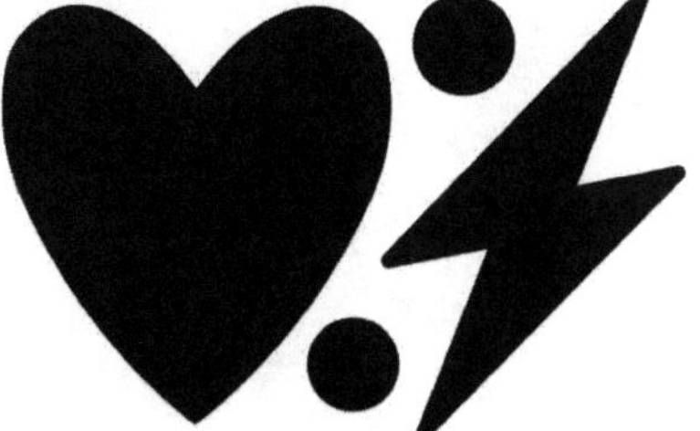

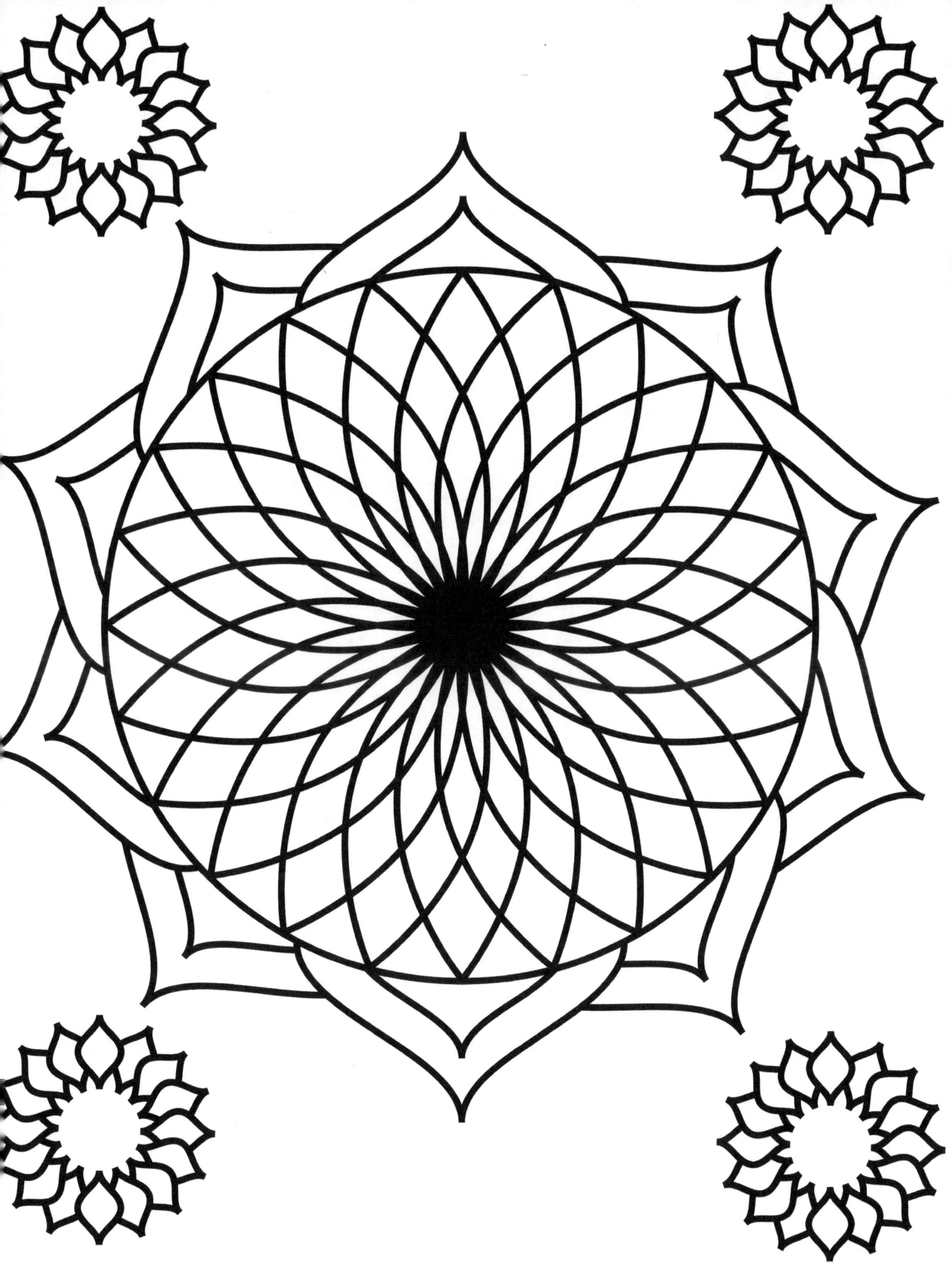

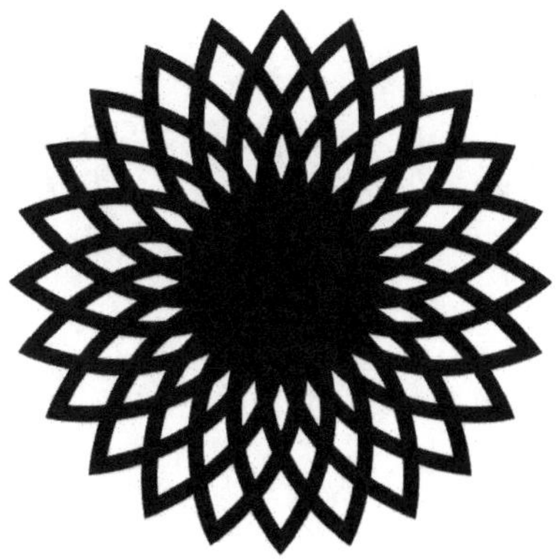

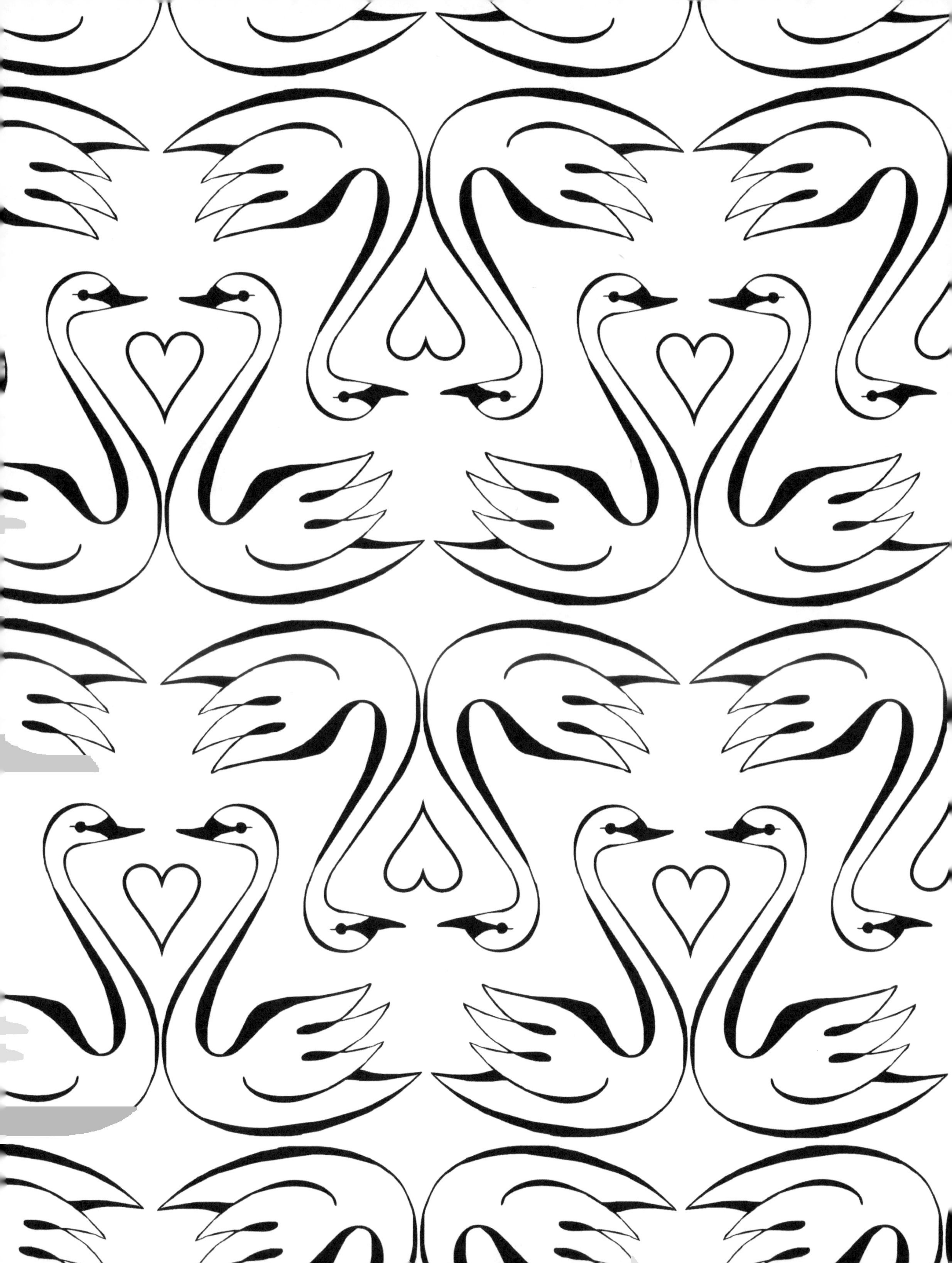

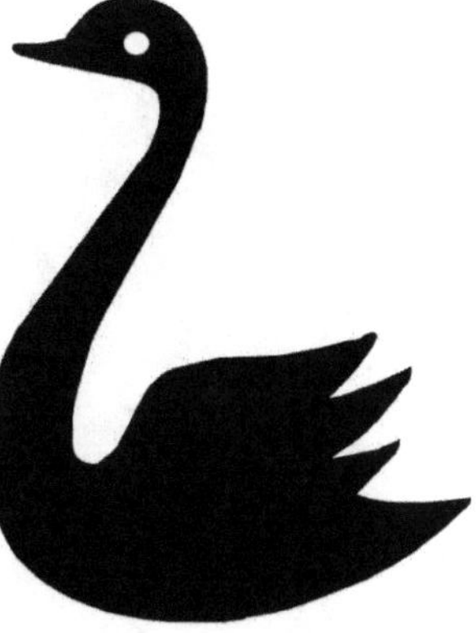

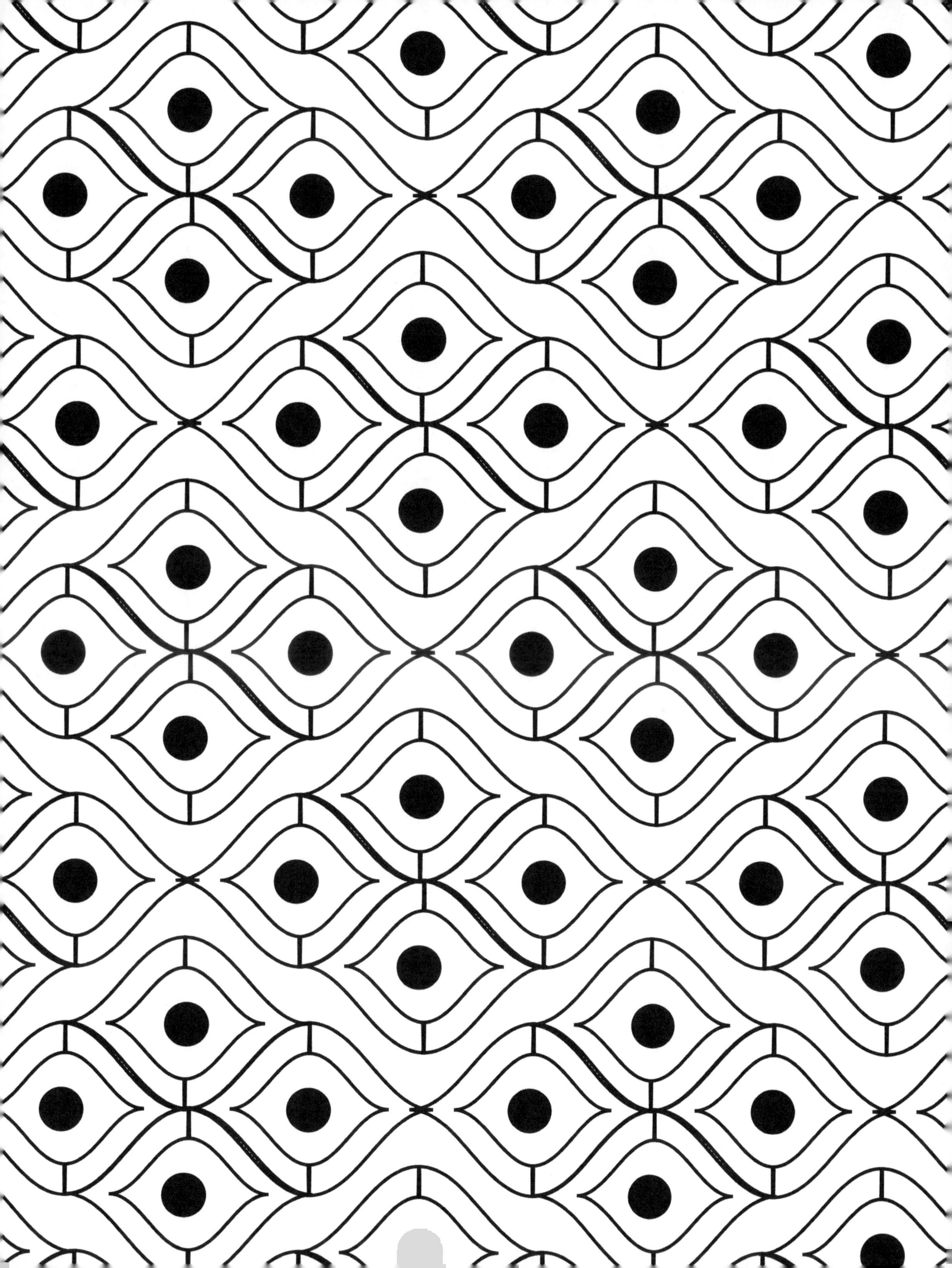

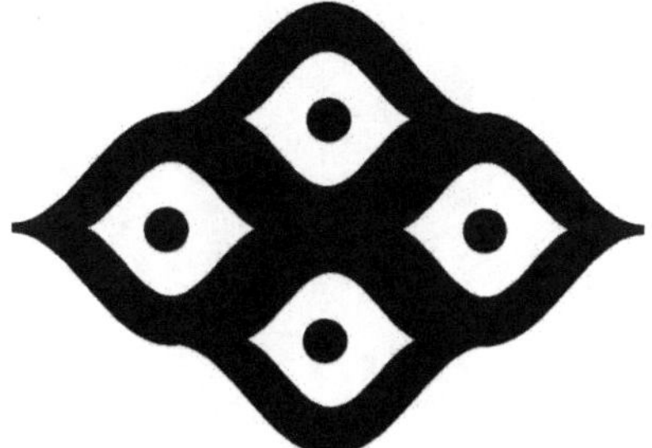

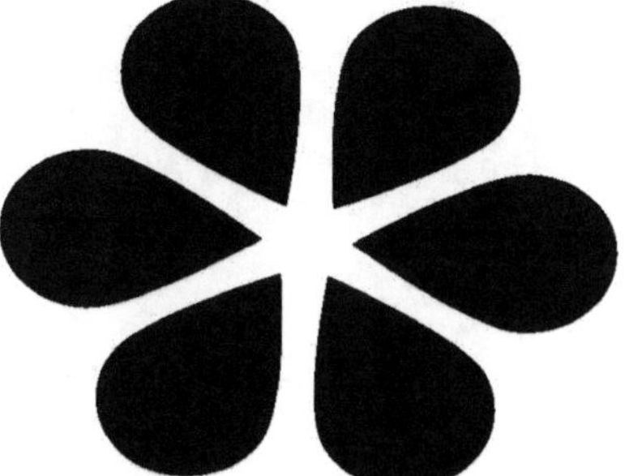

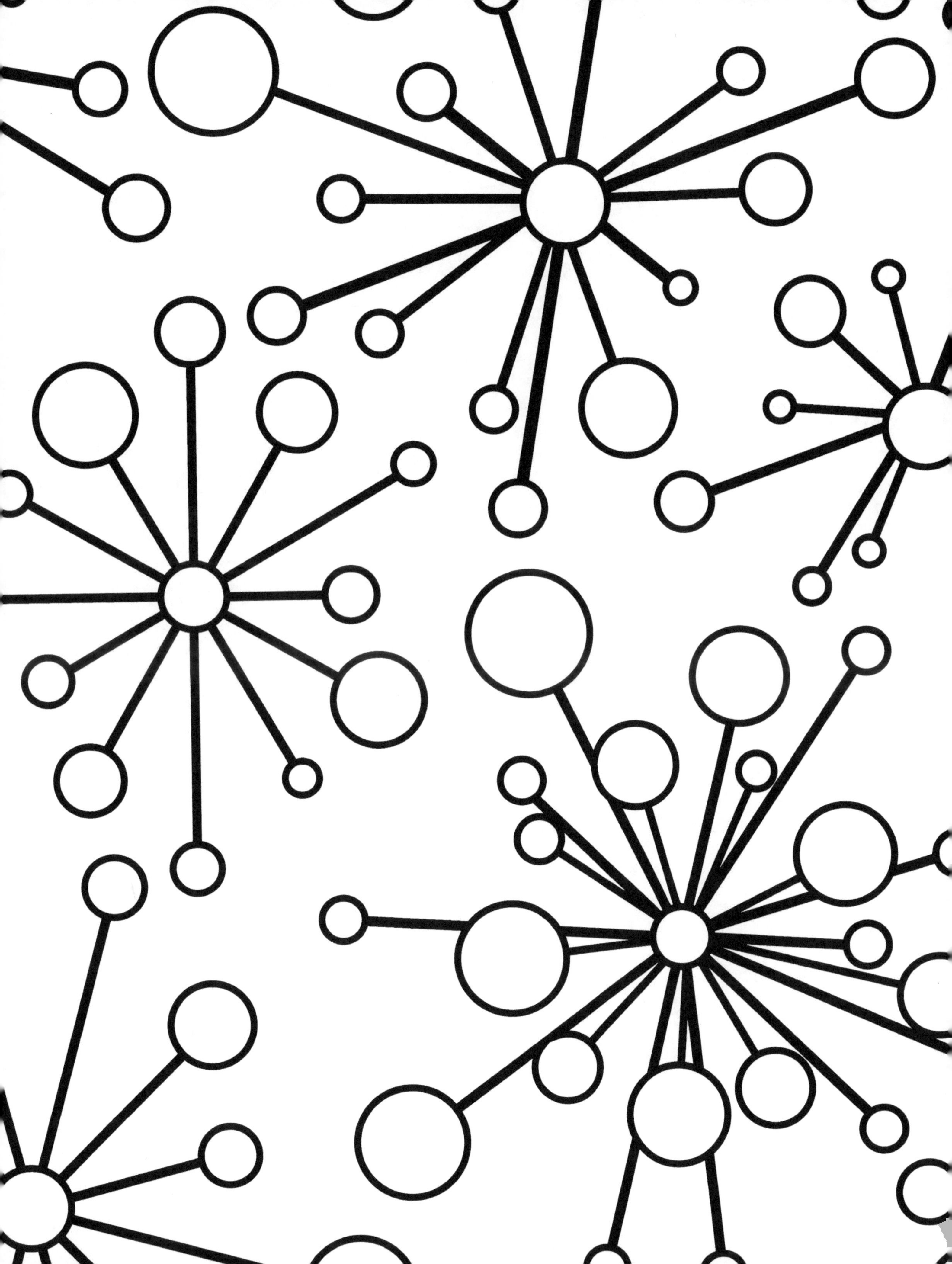

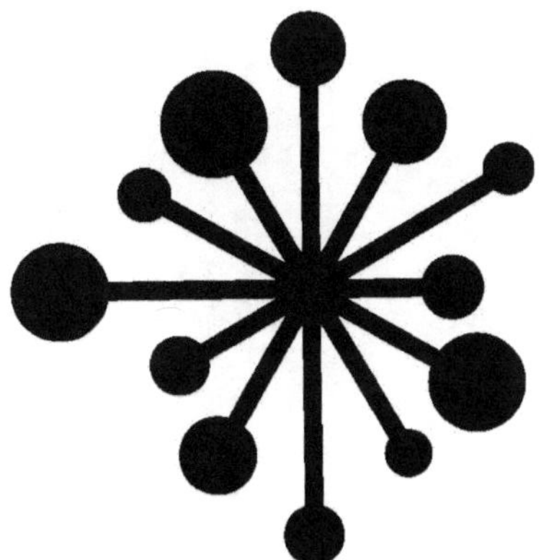

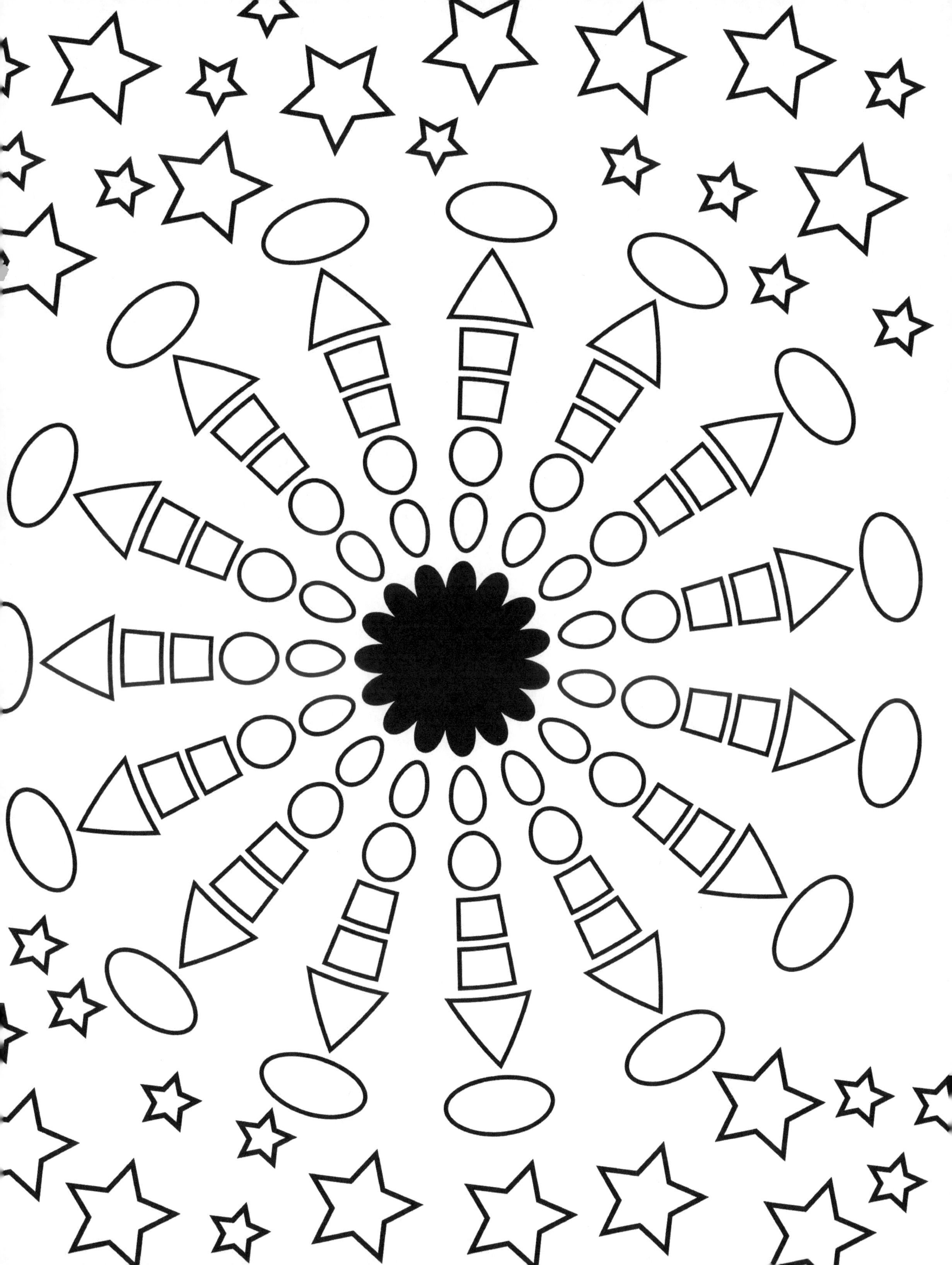

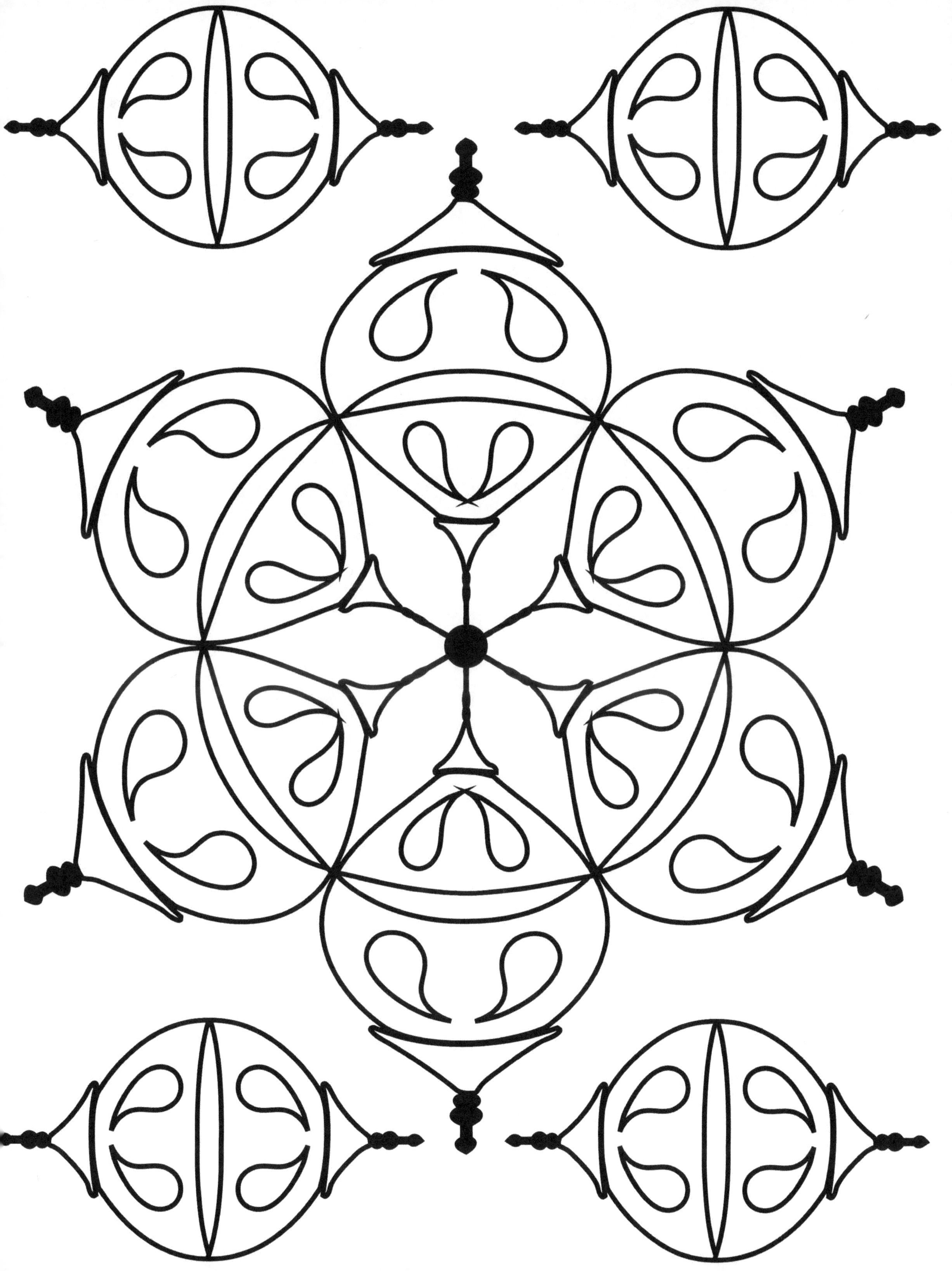

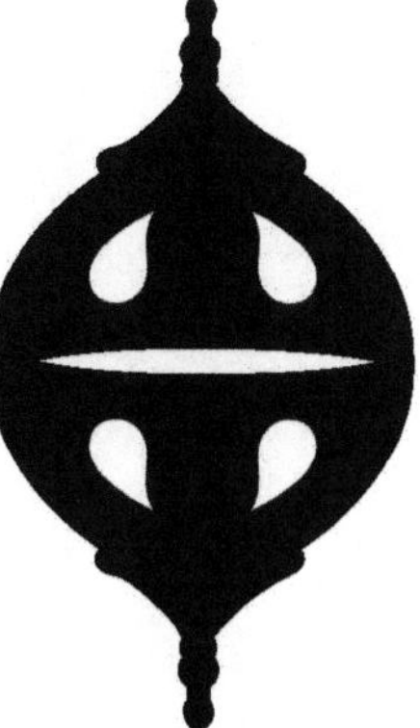

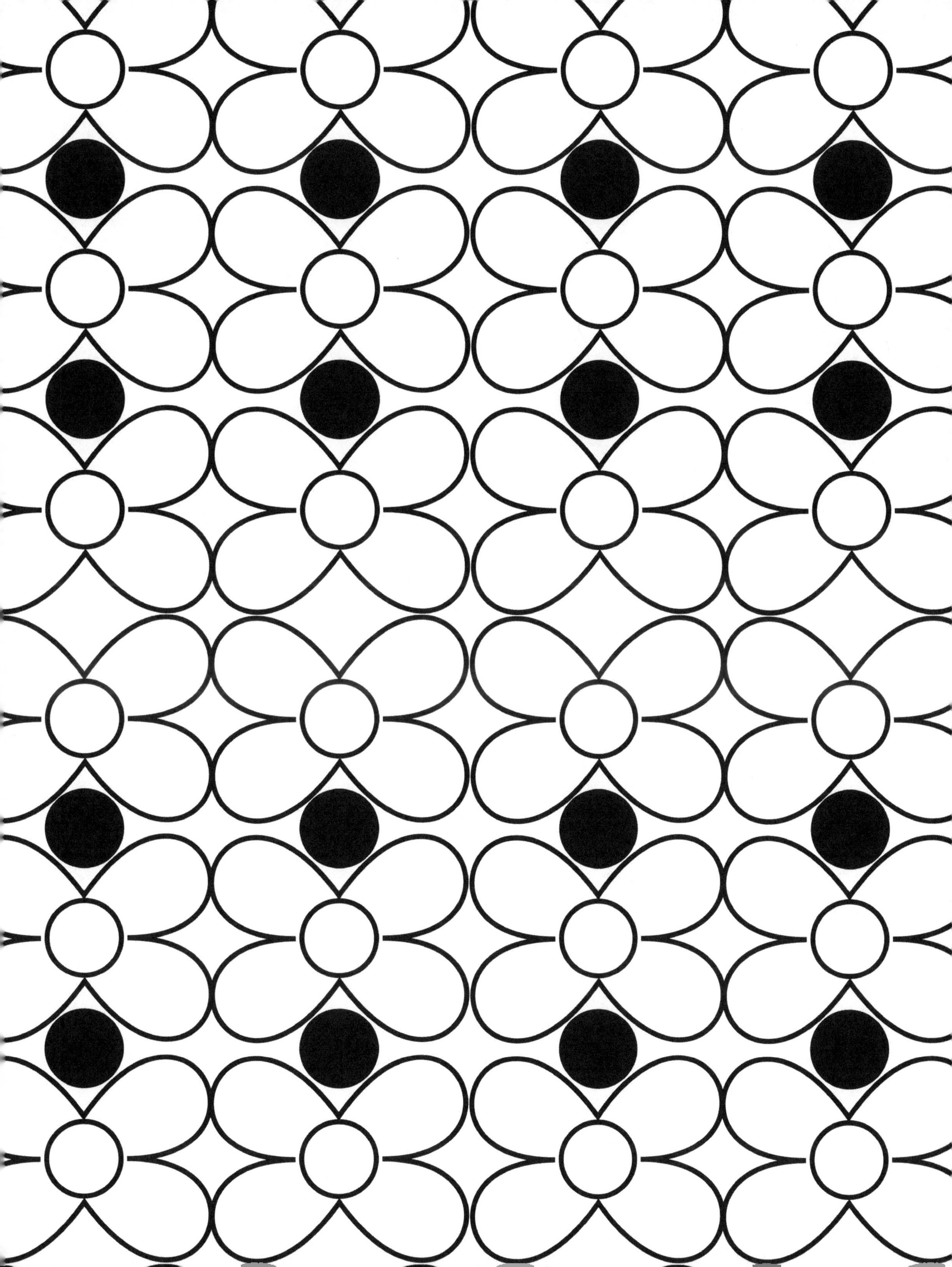

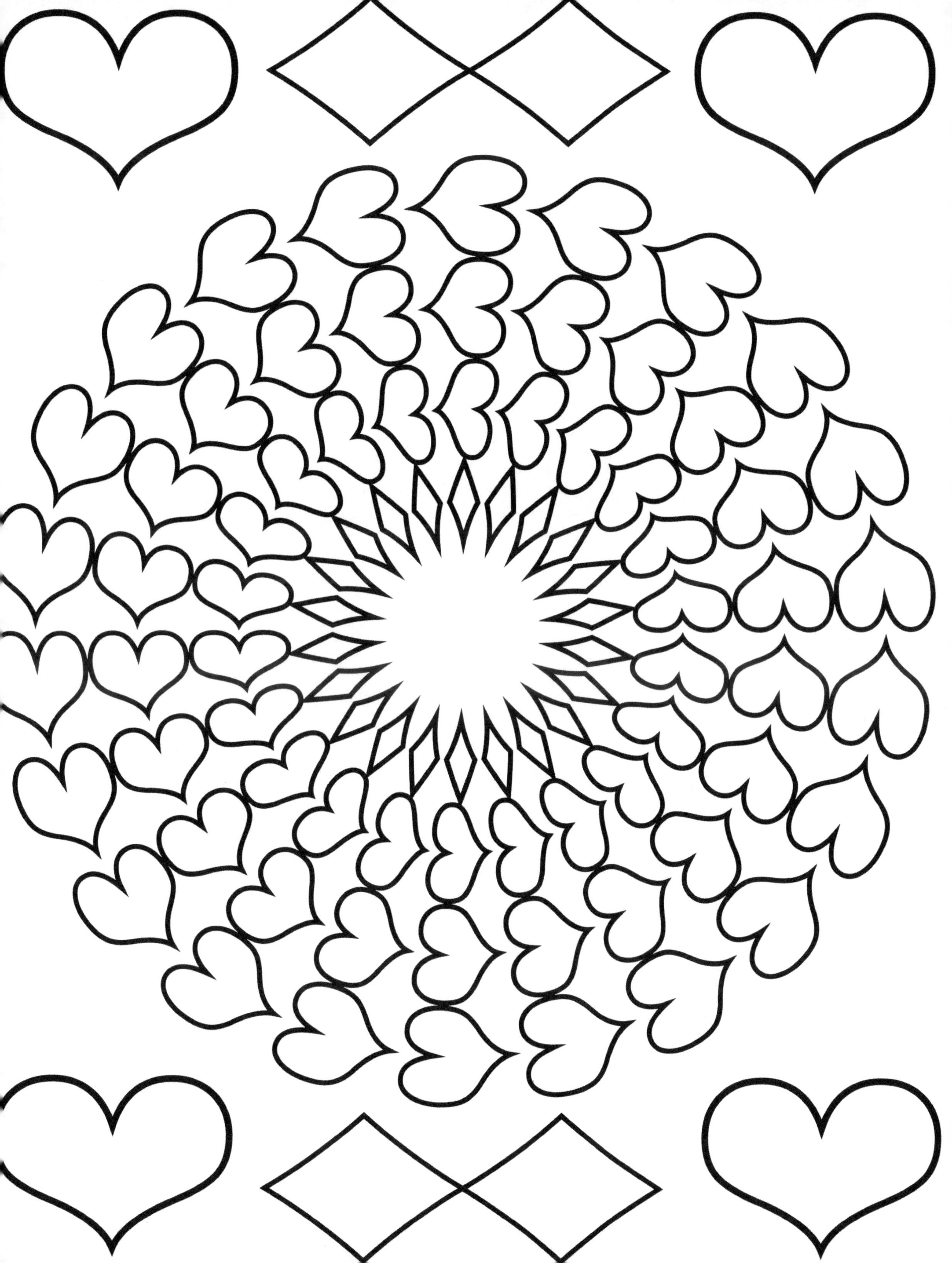

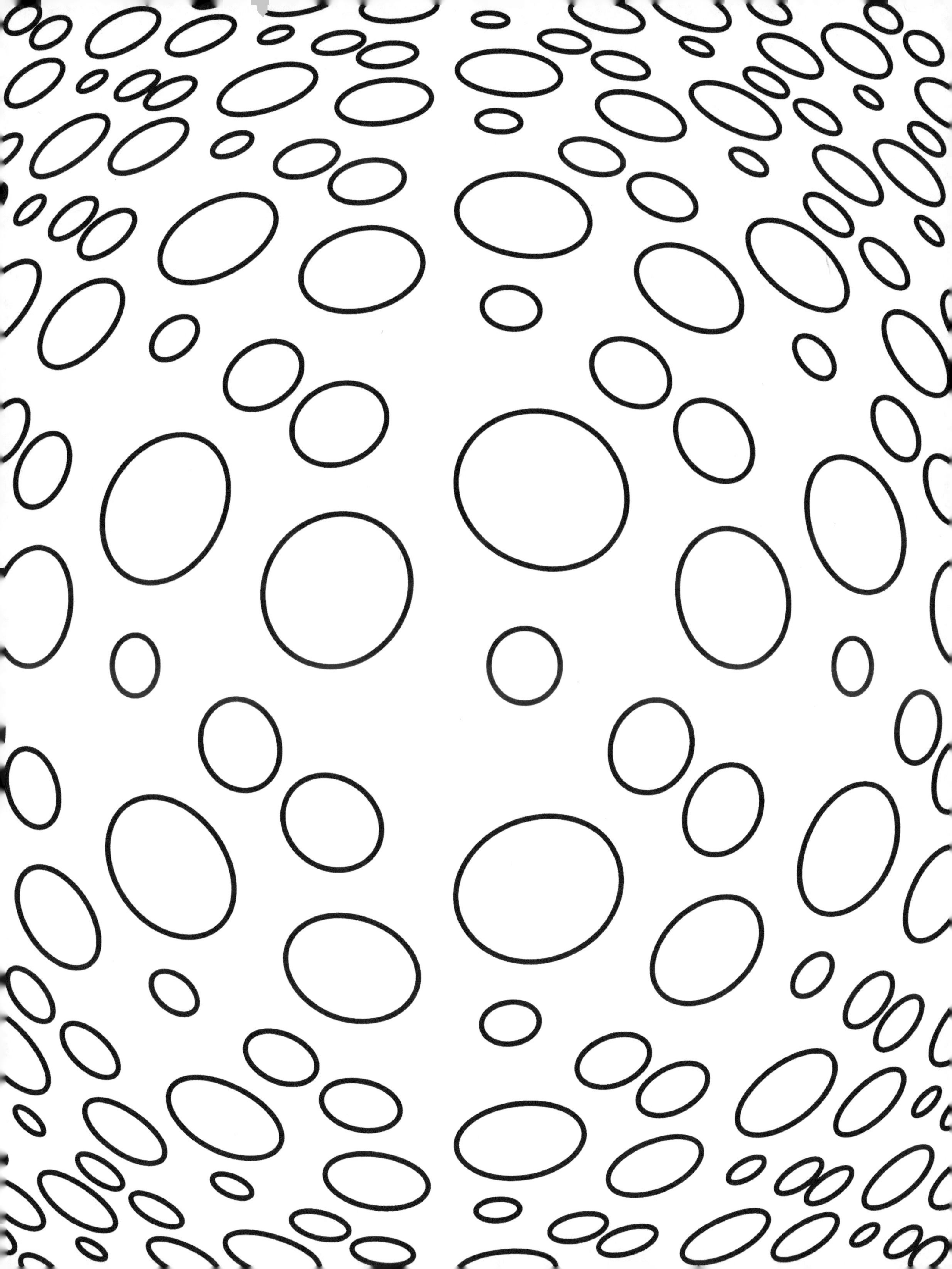

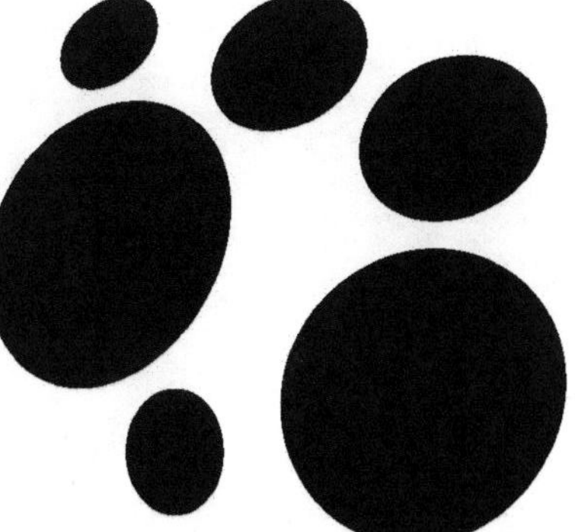

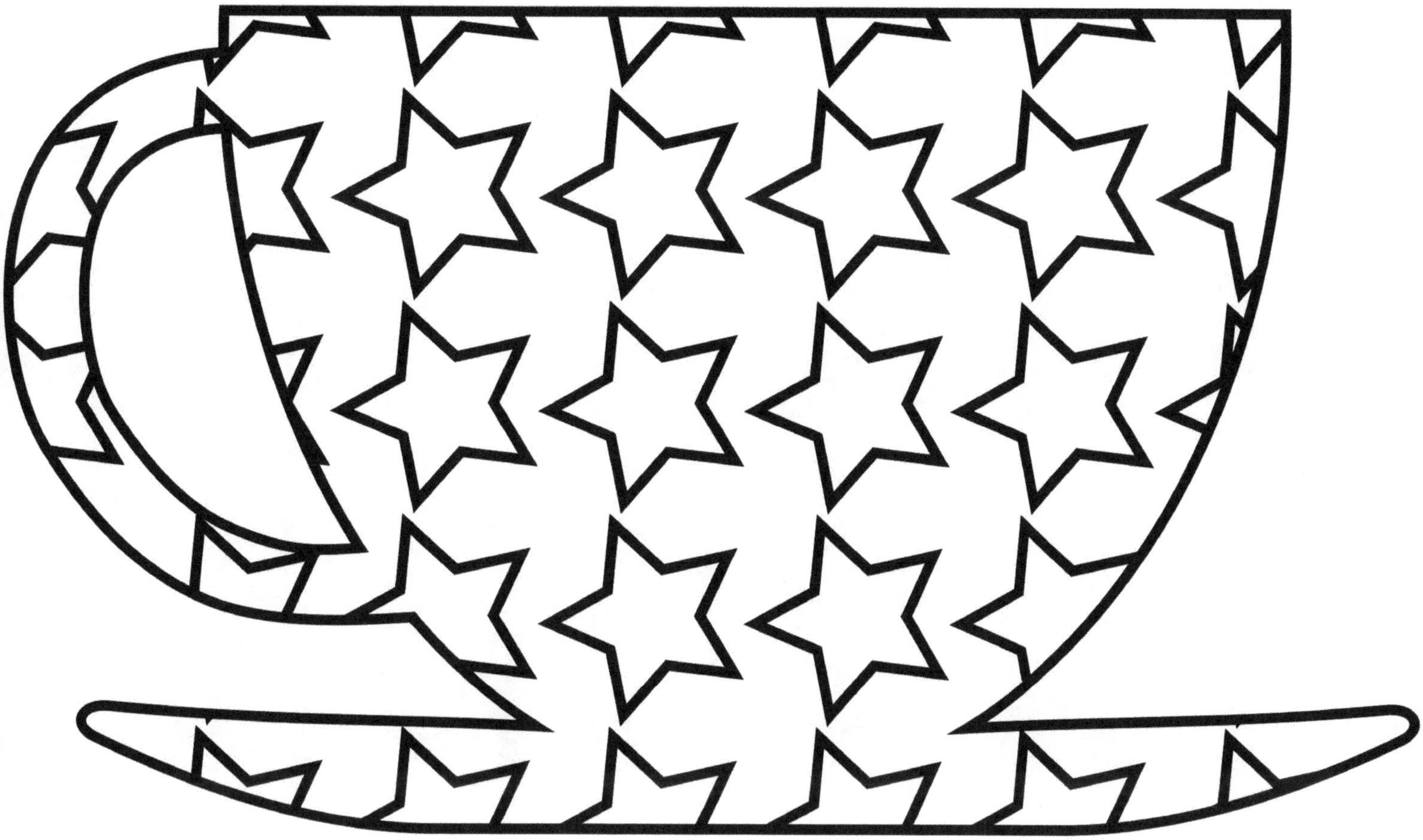

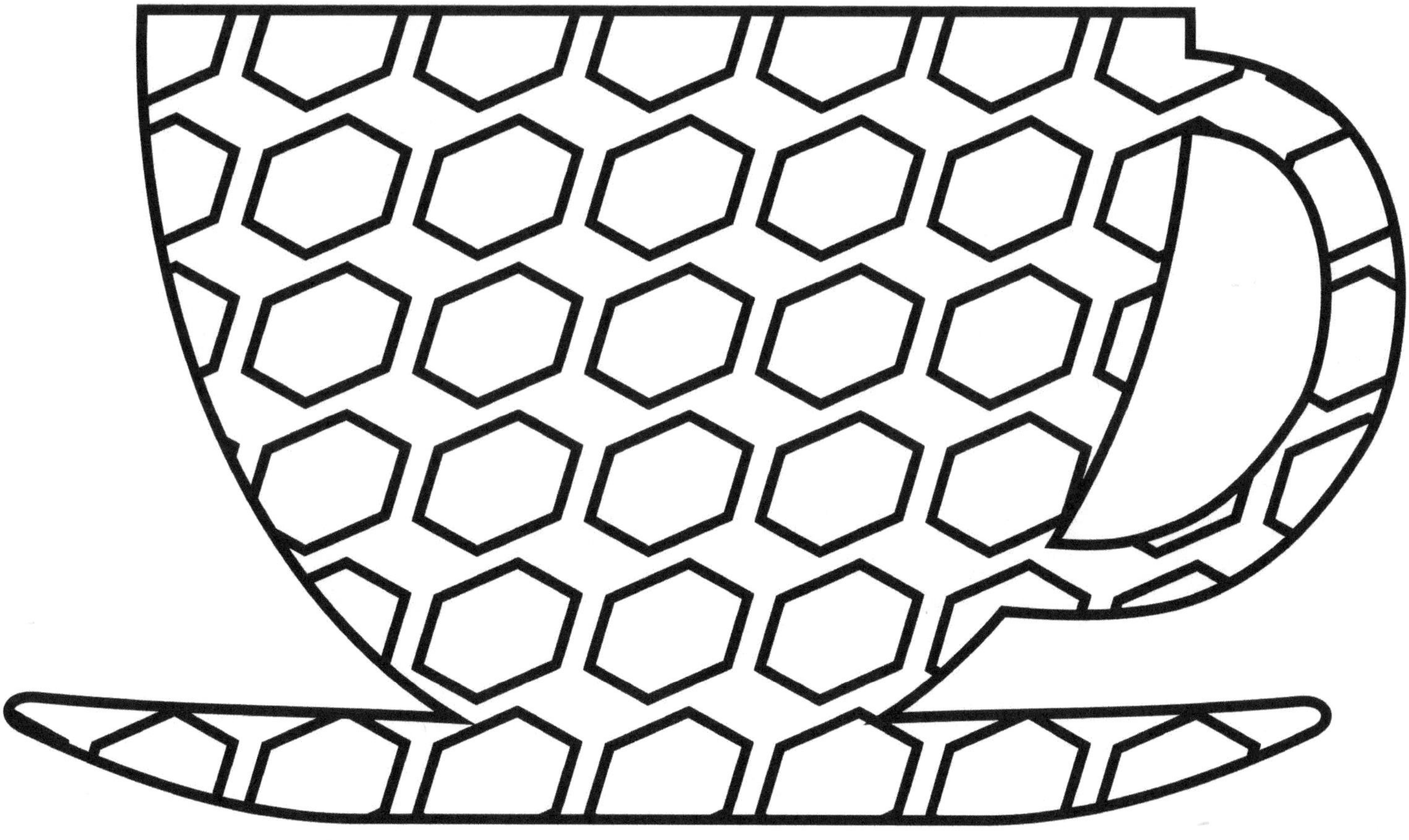

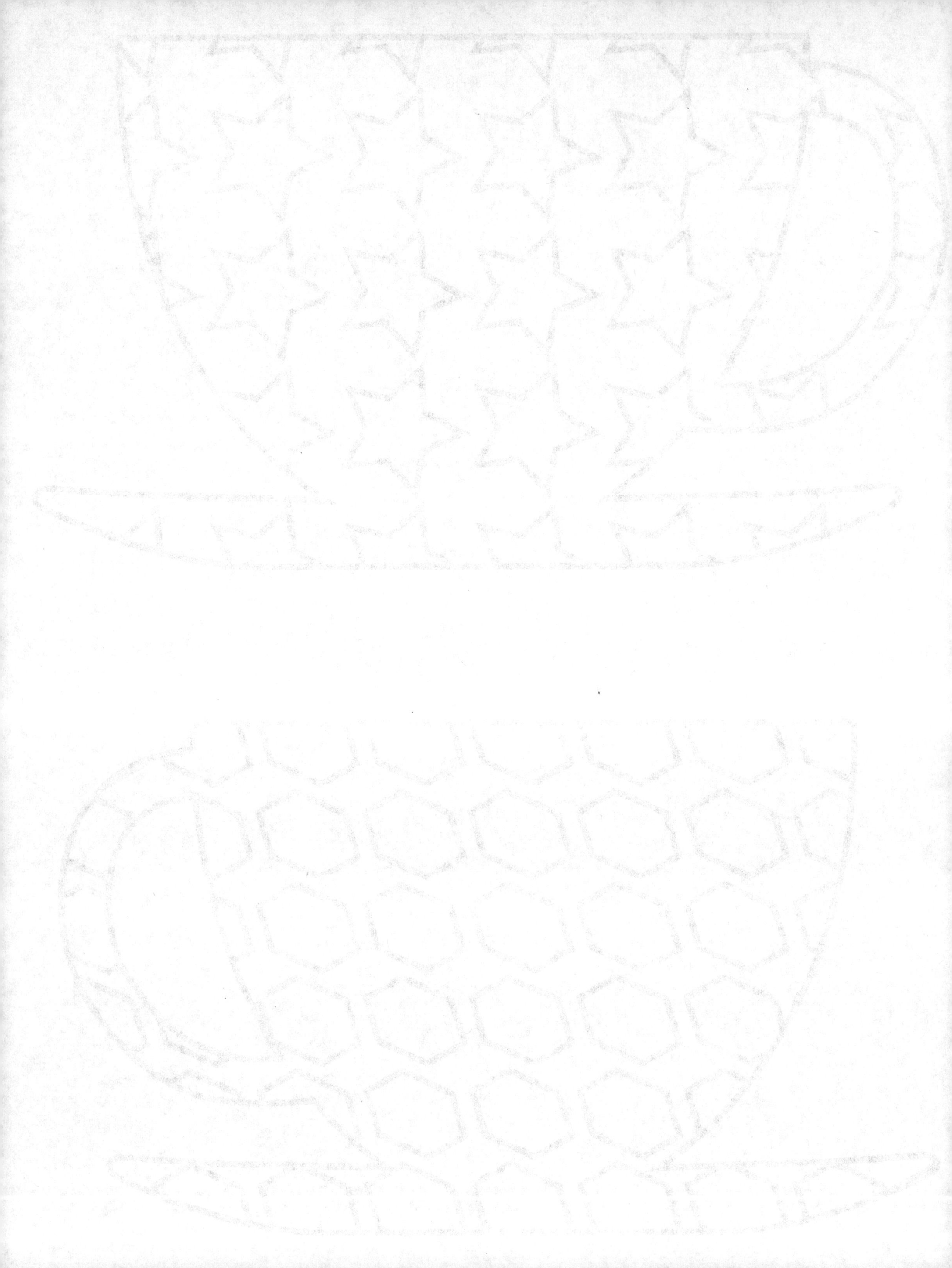

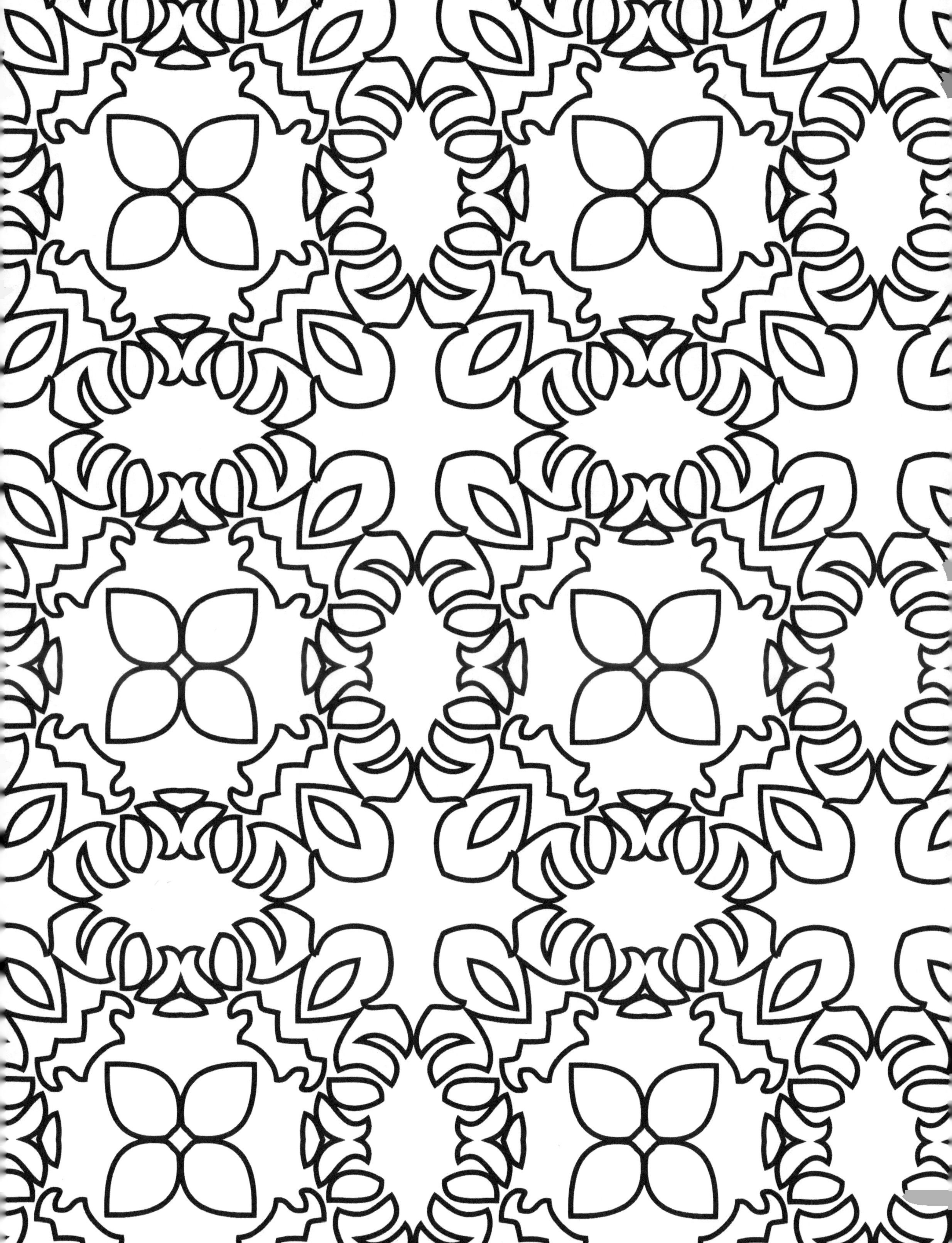

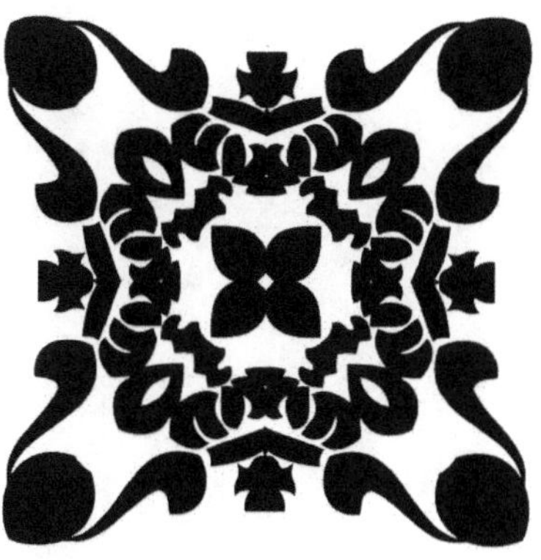

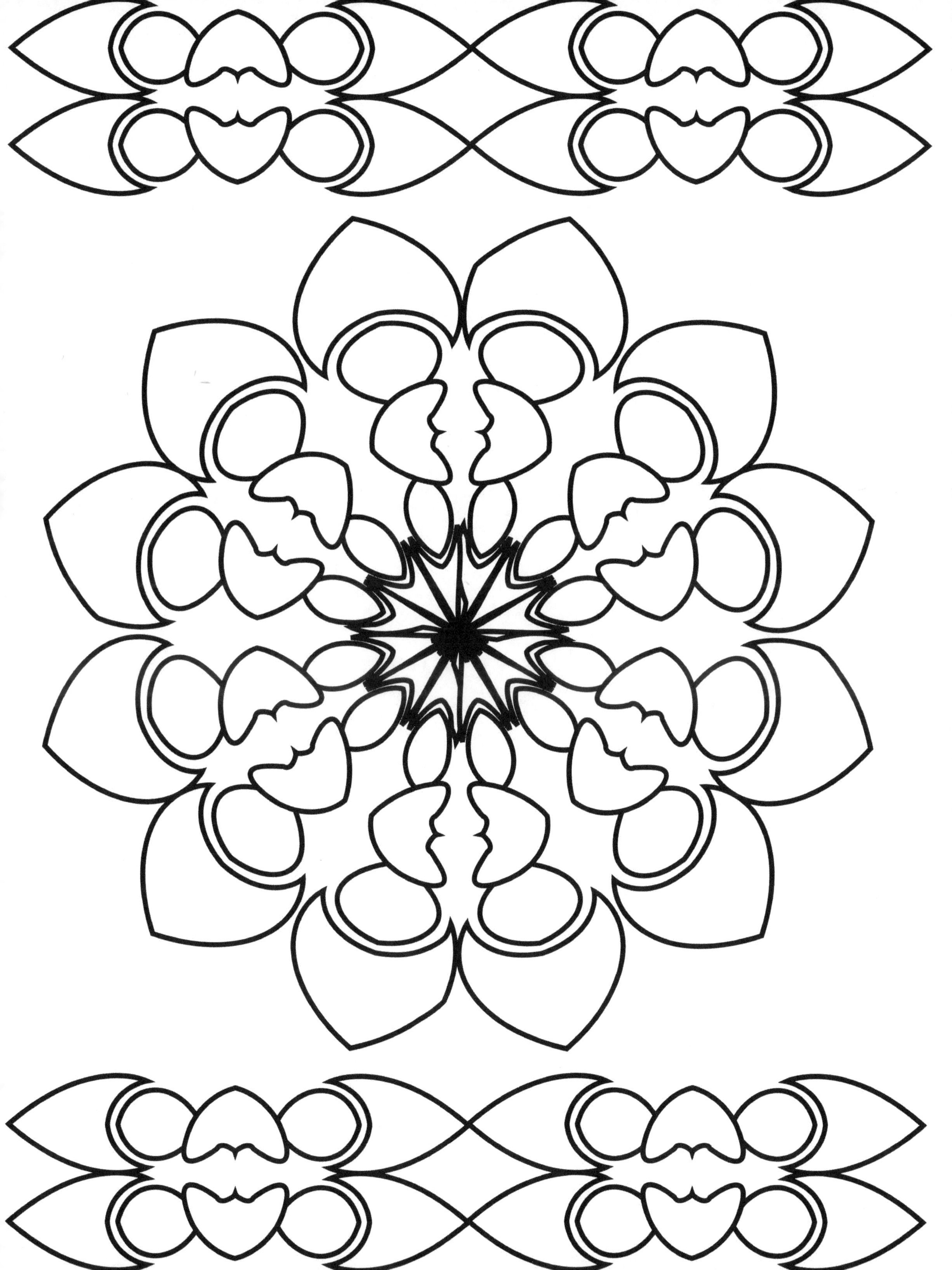

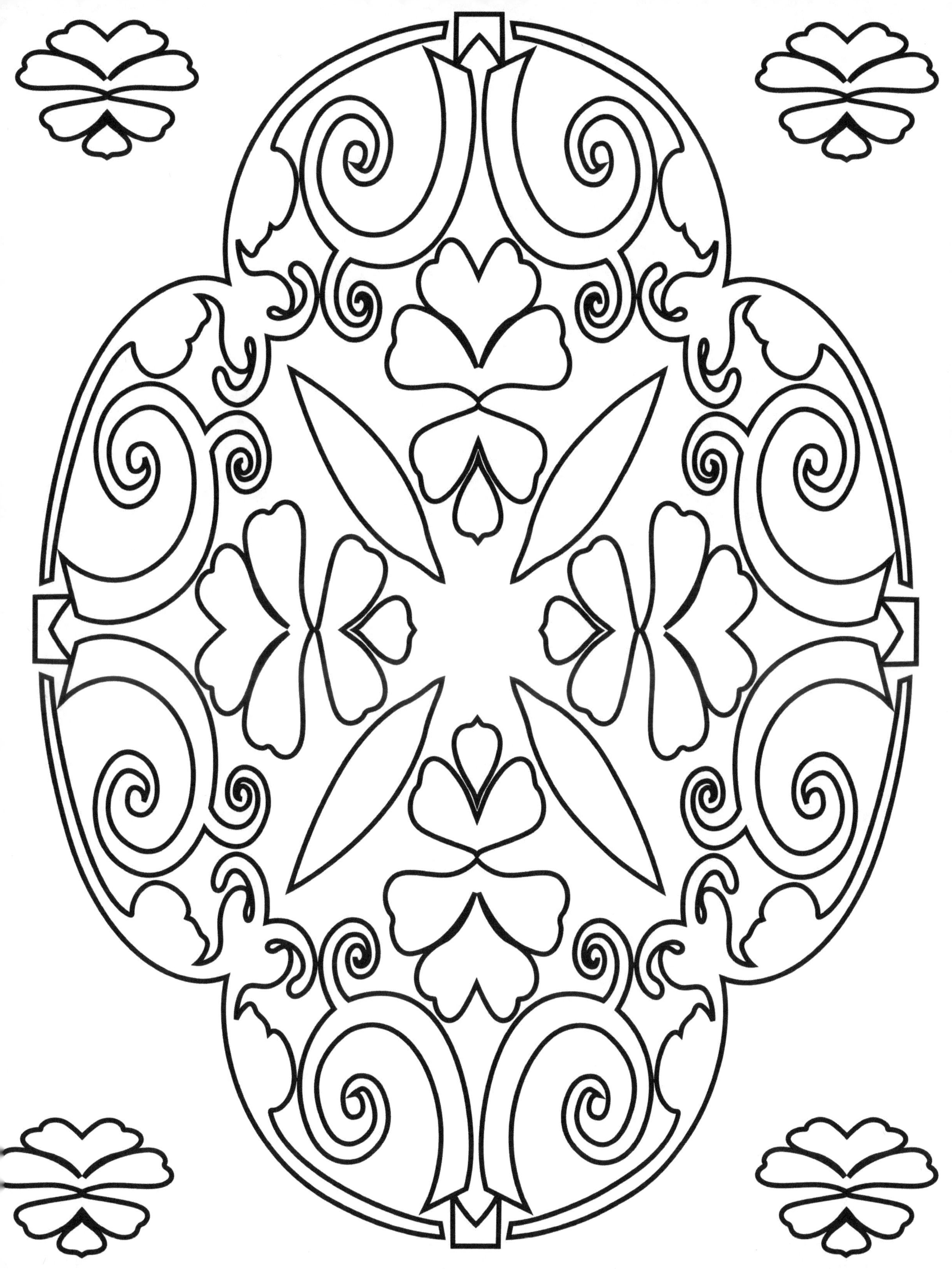

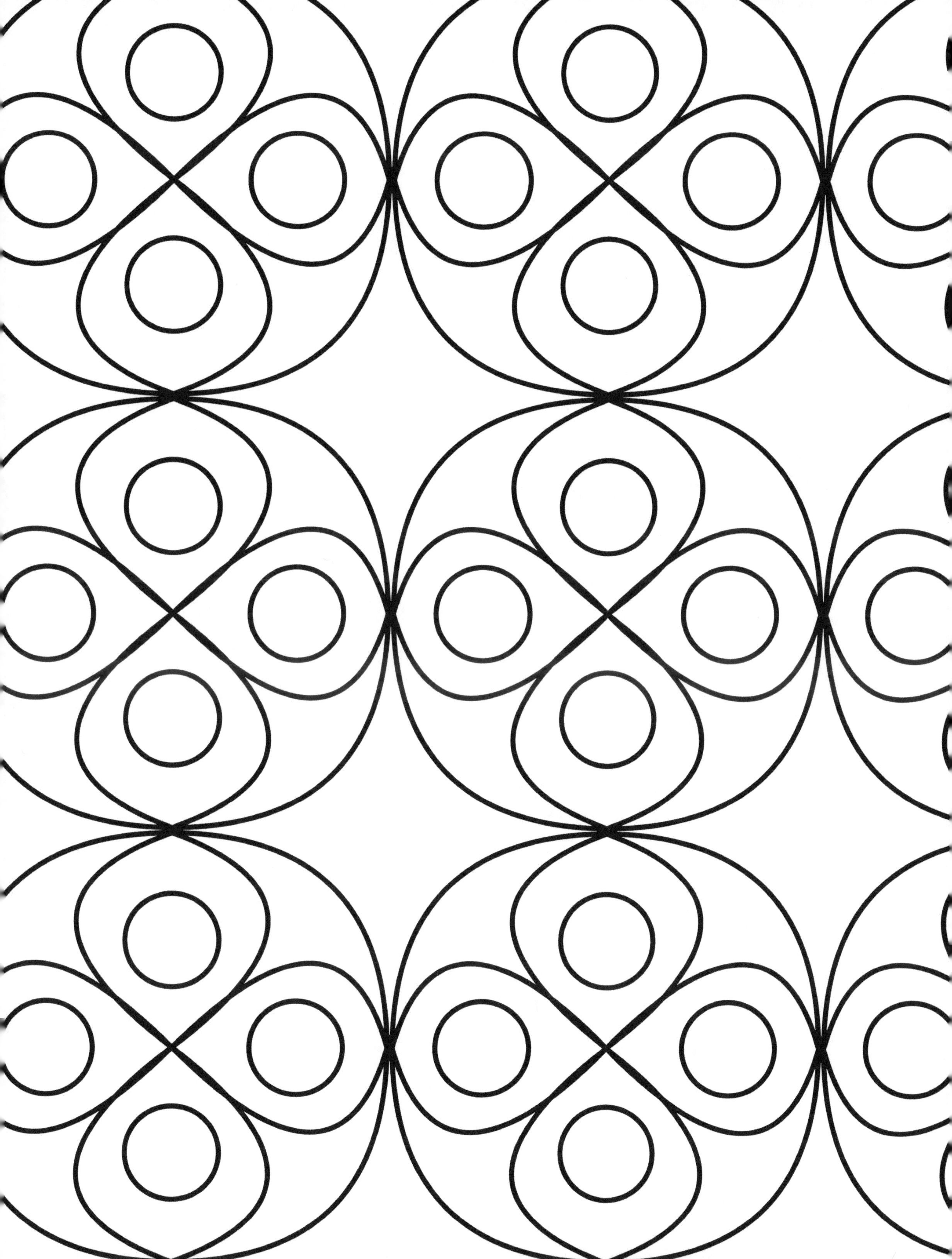

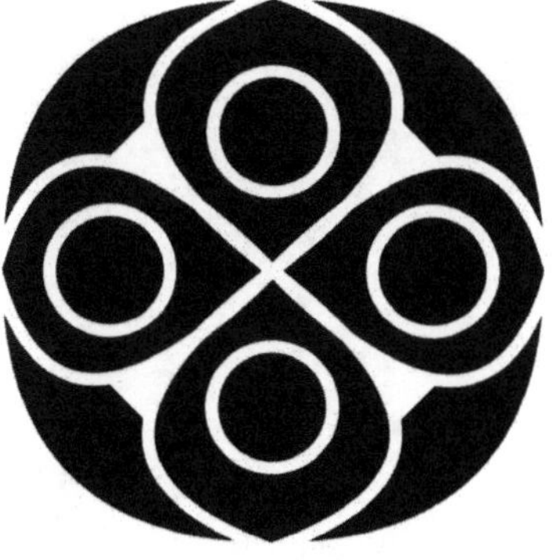

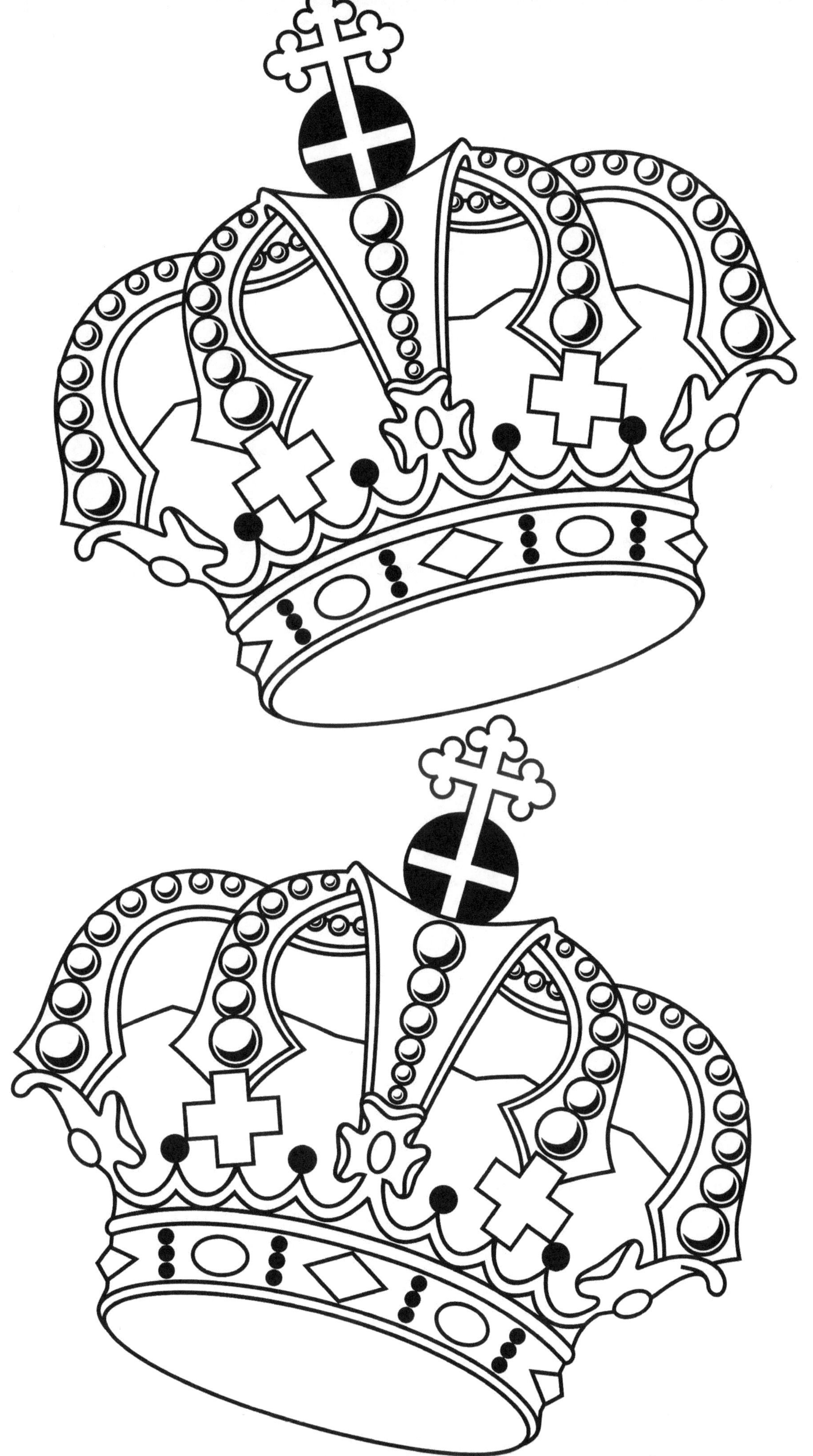

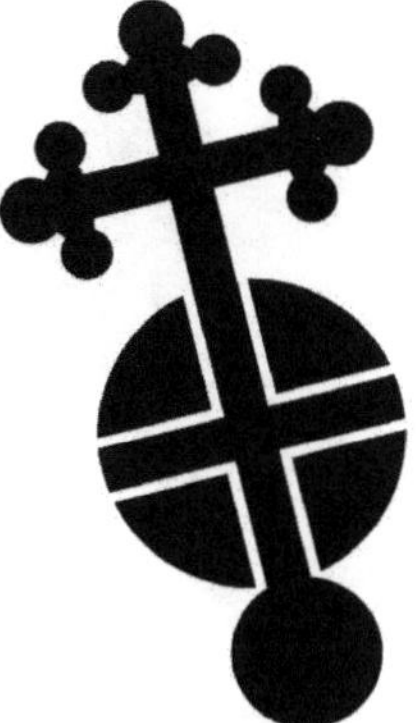

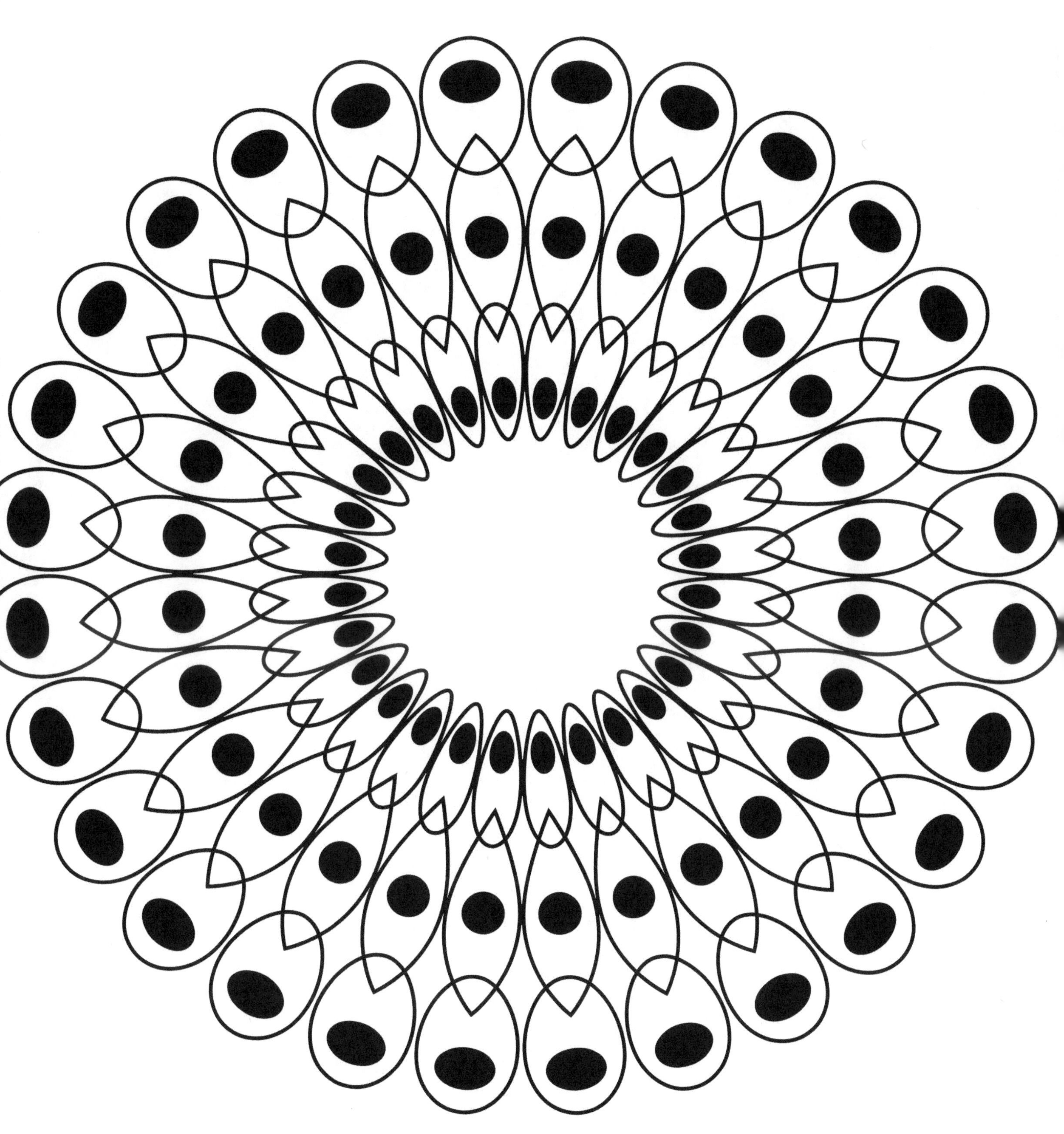

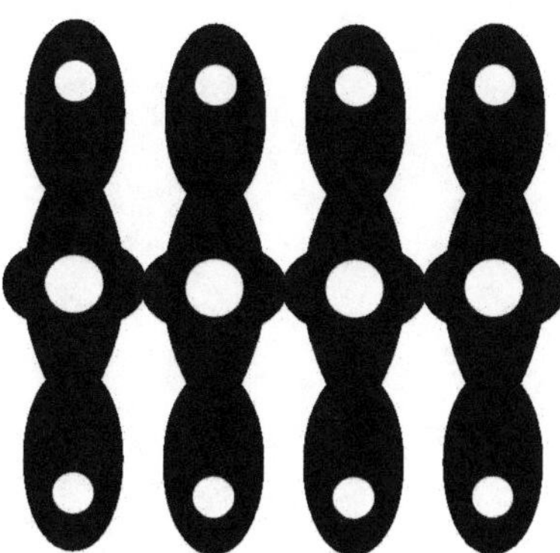

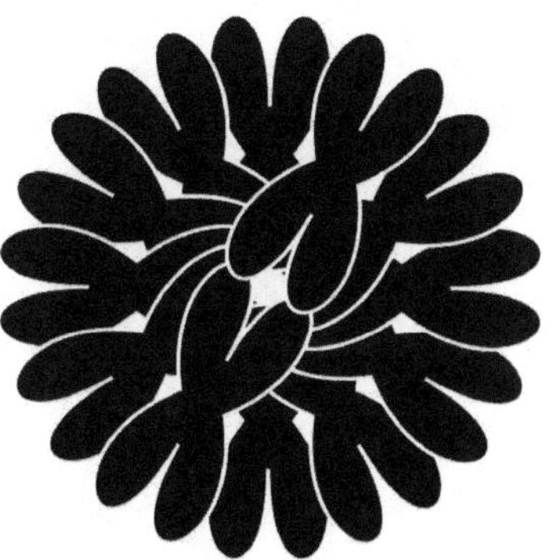

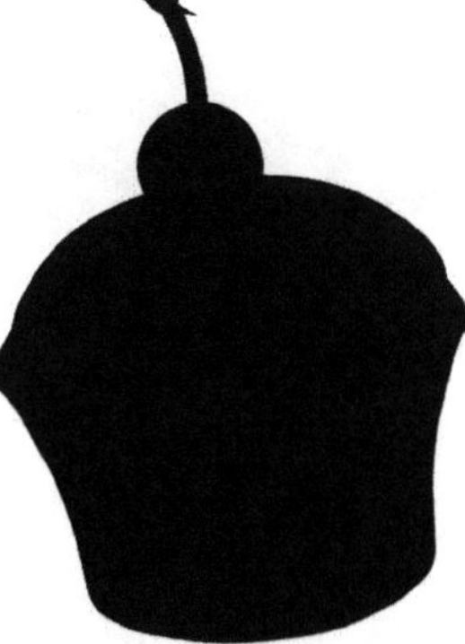

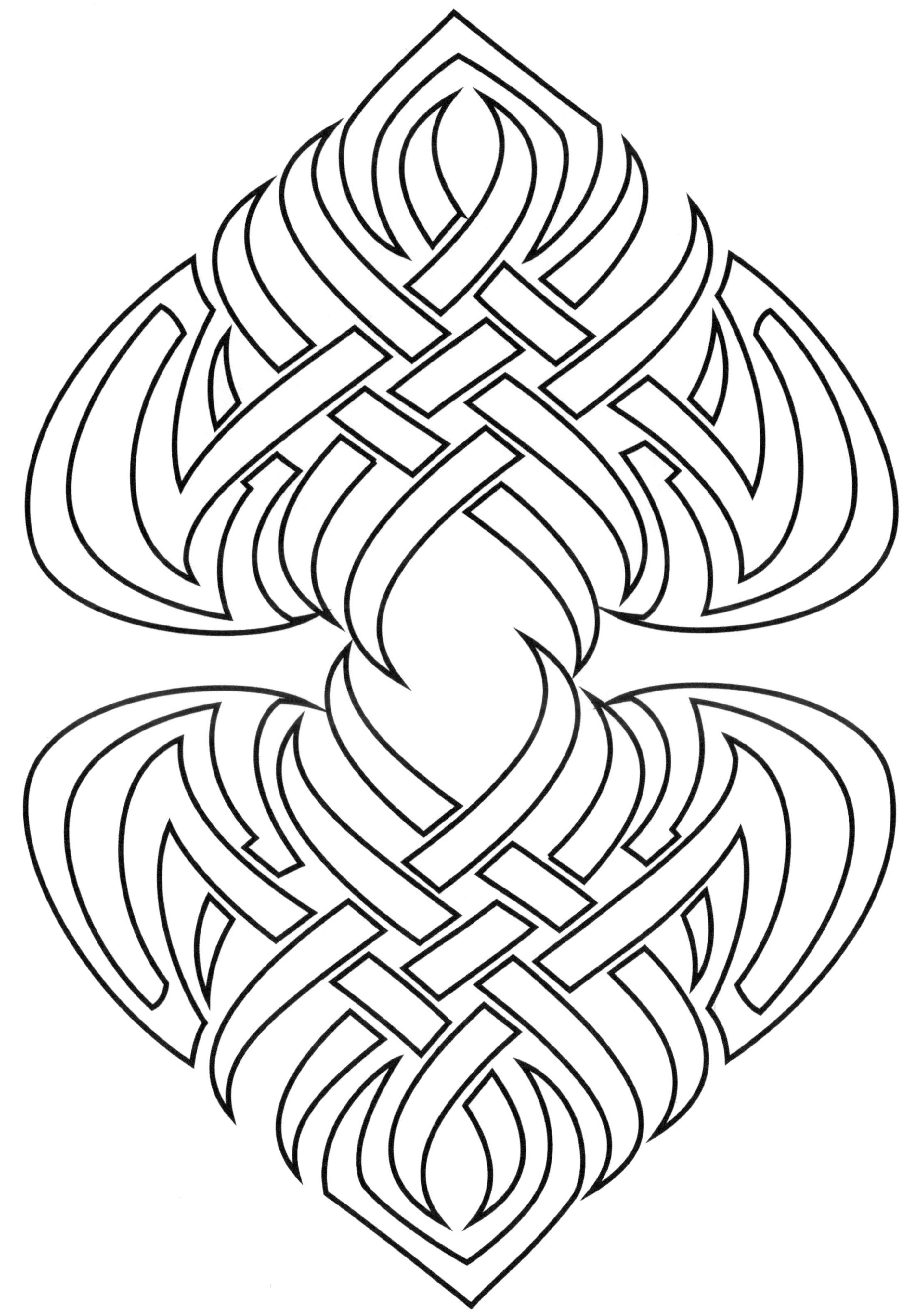

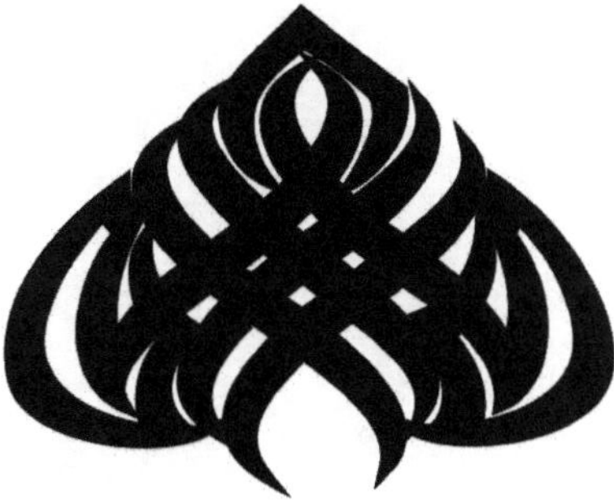

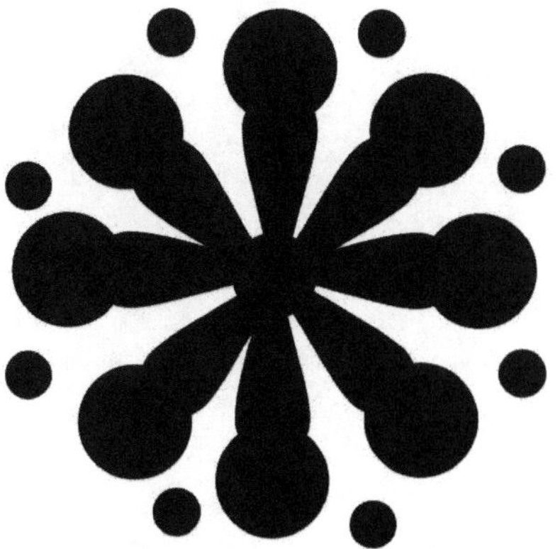

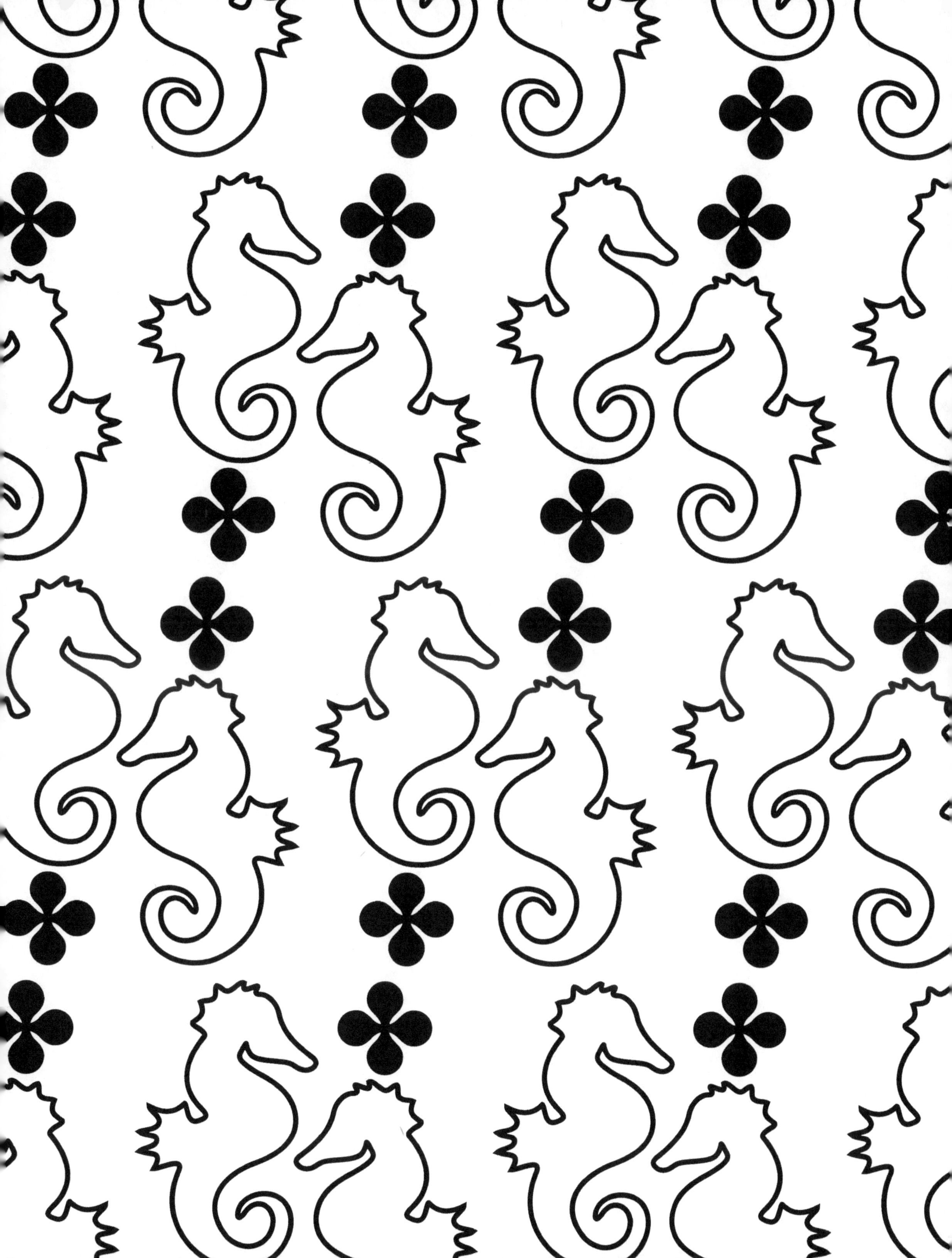

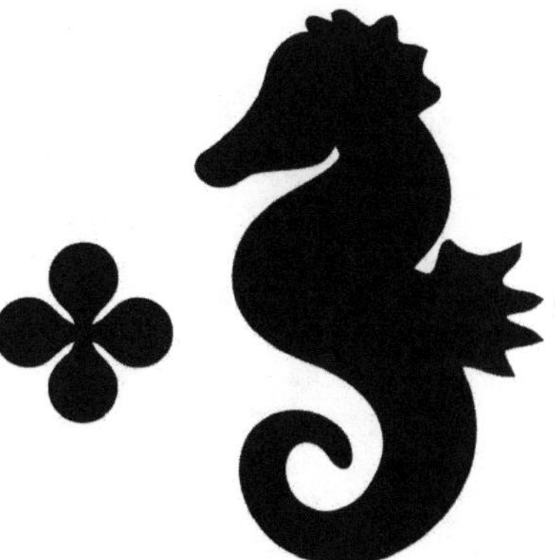

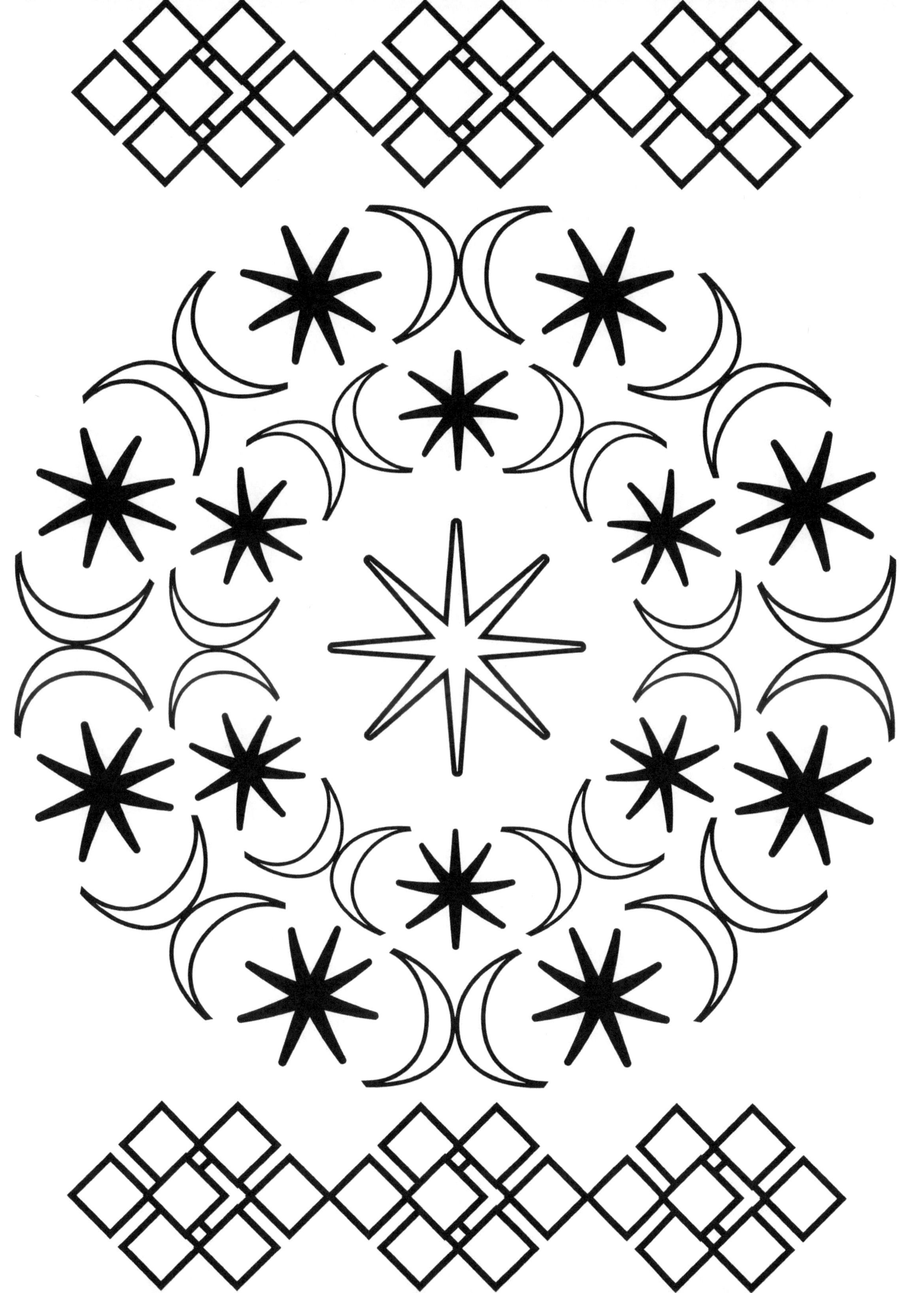

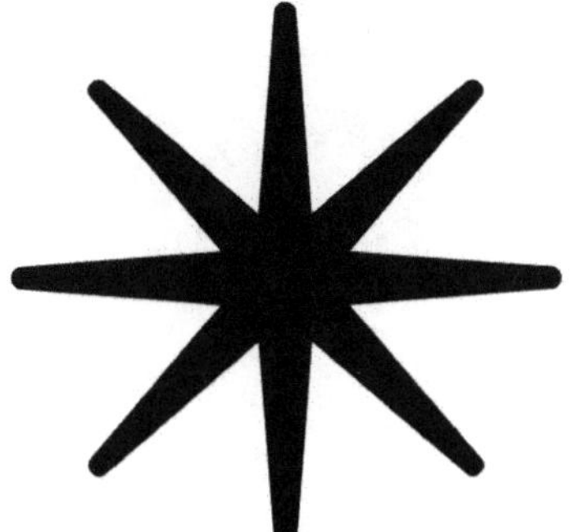

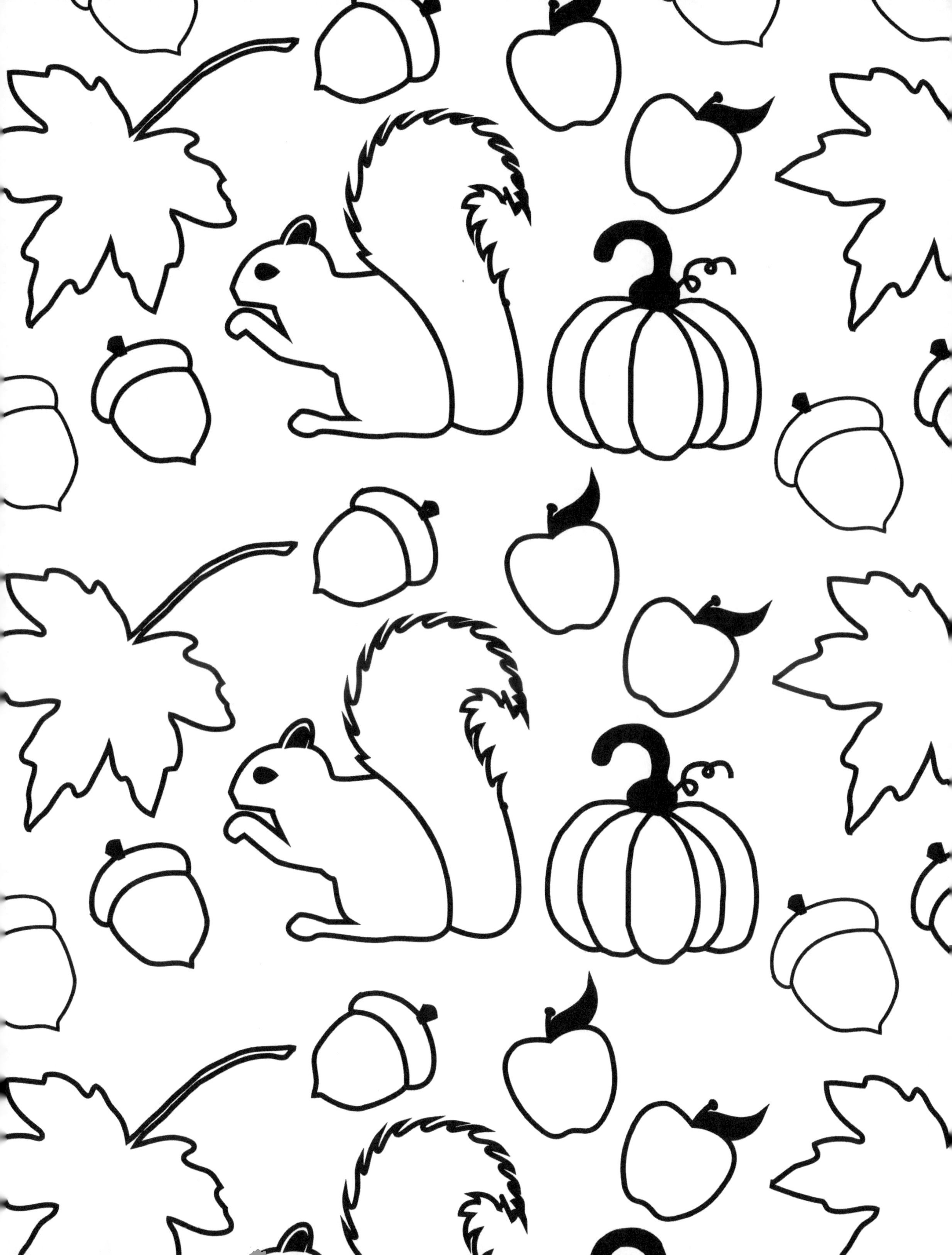

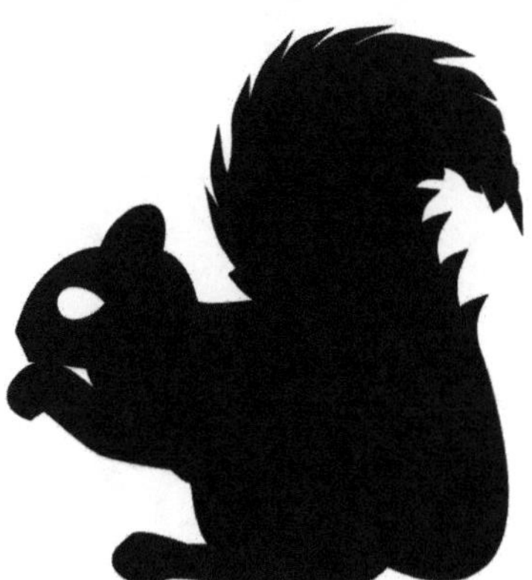

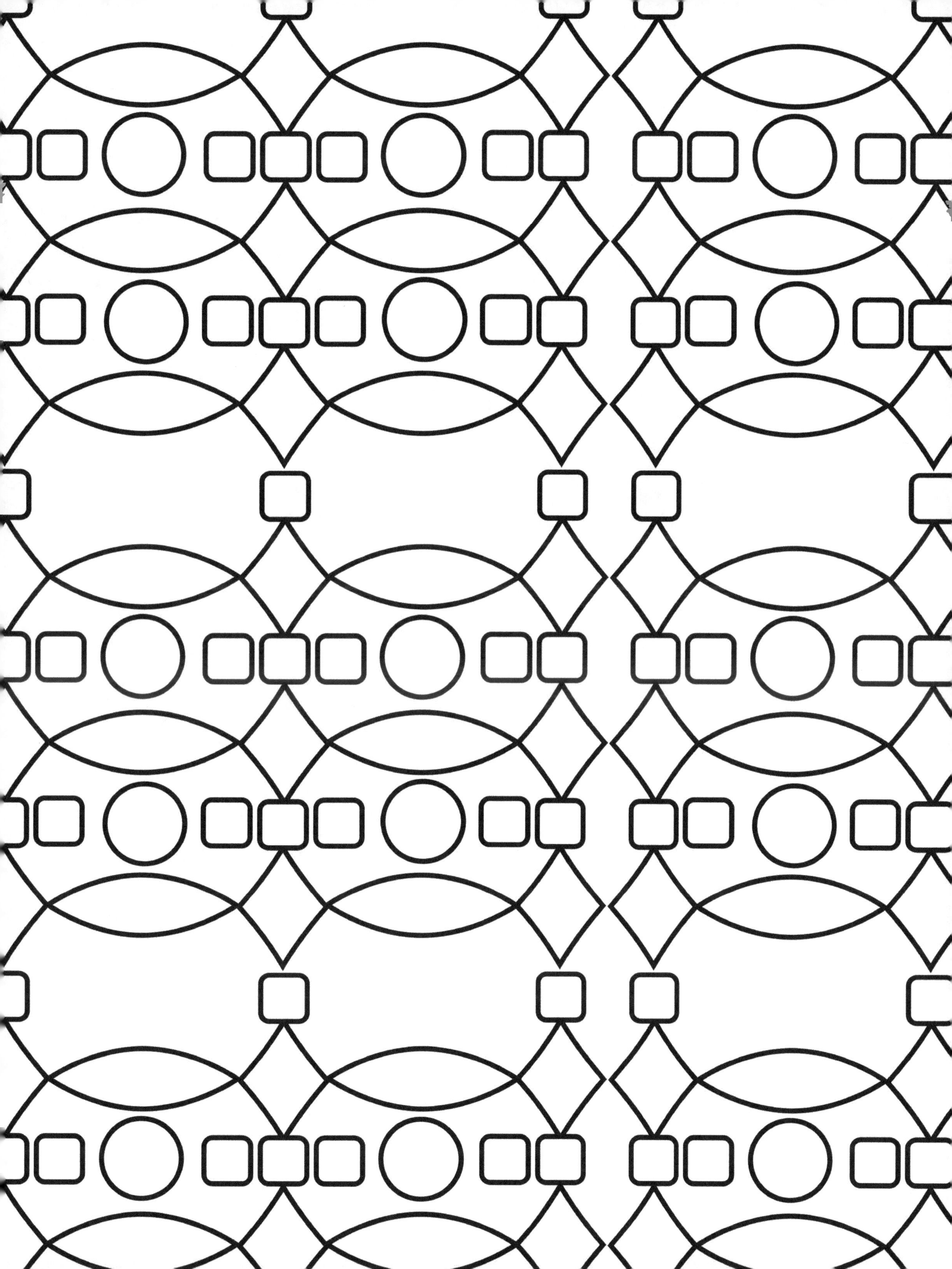

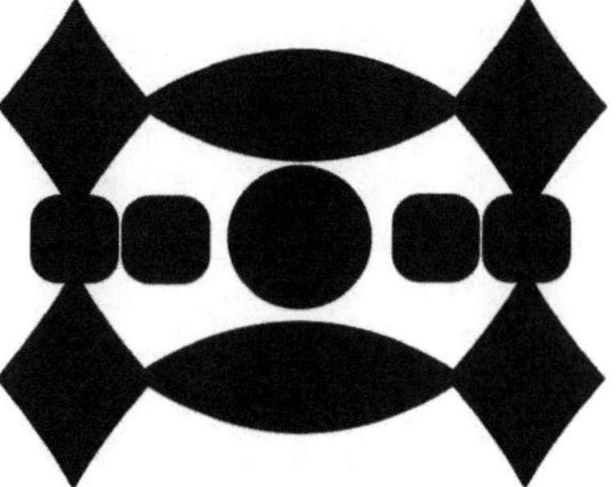

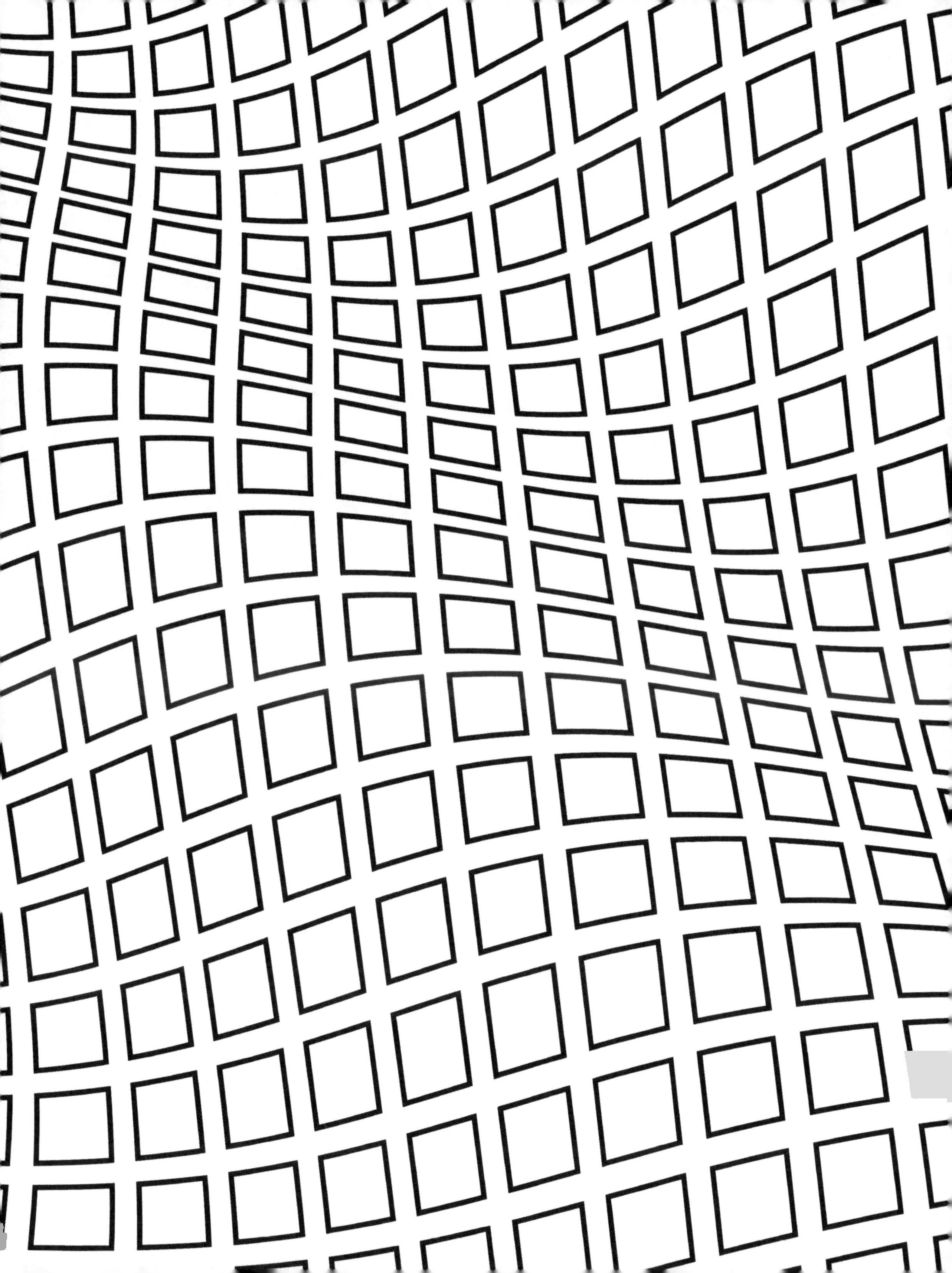

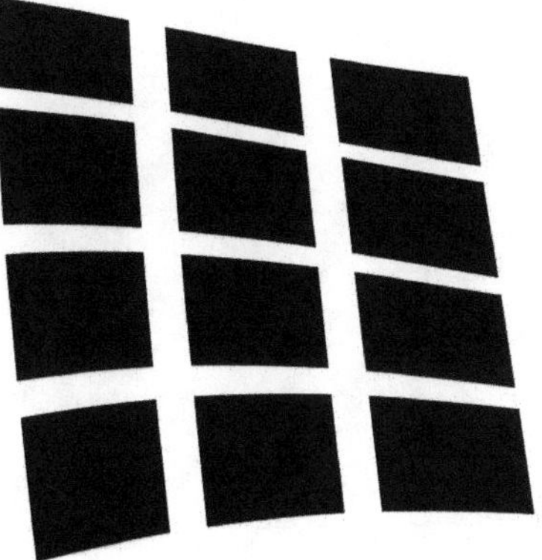

Check out our complete line of coloring books and upcoming products at unplugcoloring.com.

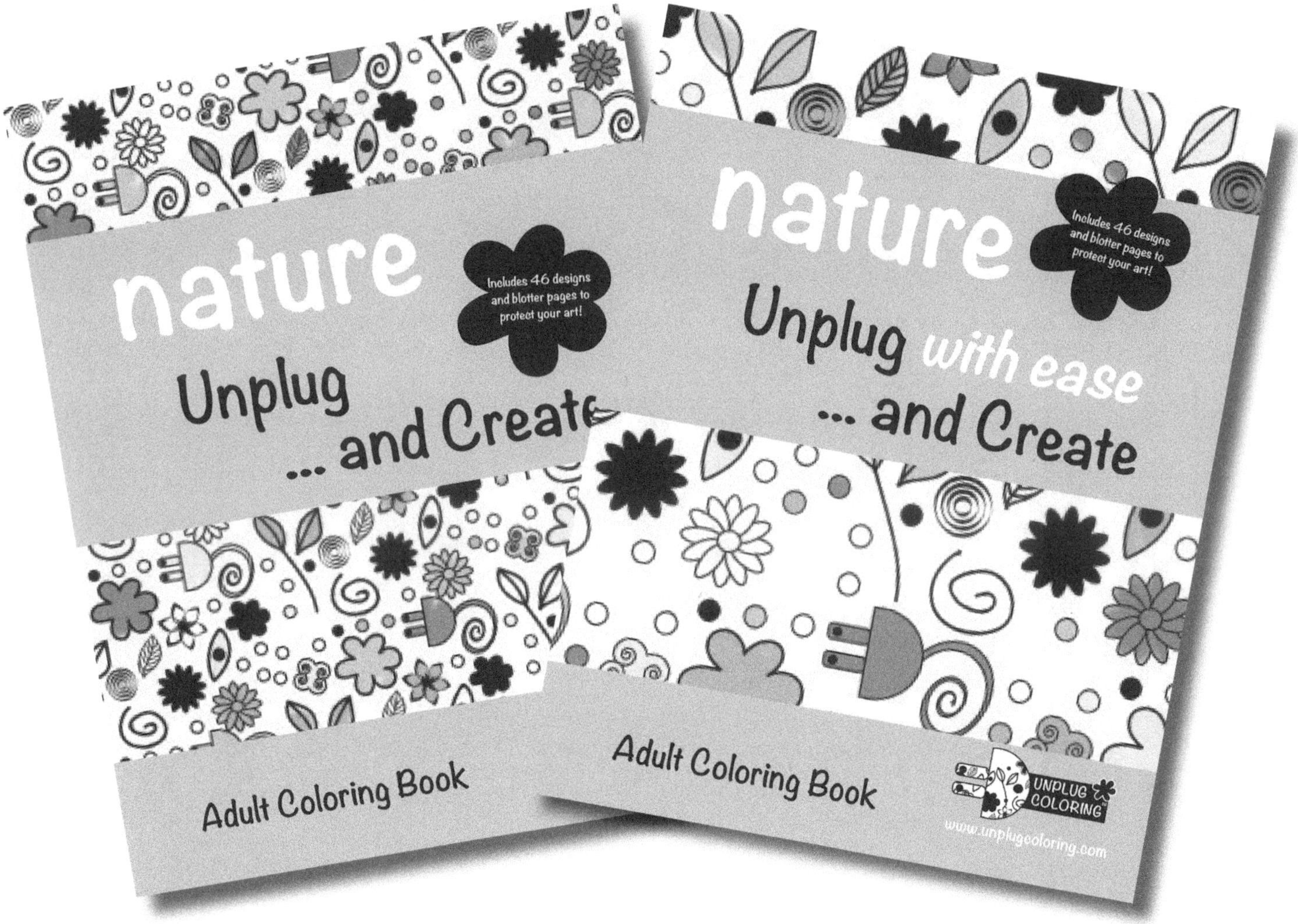

nature
Includes 46 designs and blotter pages to protect your art!
Unplug ... and Create
Adult Coloring Book

nature
Includes 46 designs and blotter pages to protect your art!
Unplug with ease ... and Create
Adult Coloring Book
UNPLUG COLORING
www.unplugcoloring.com

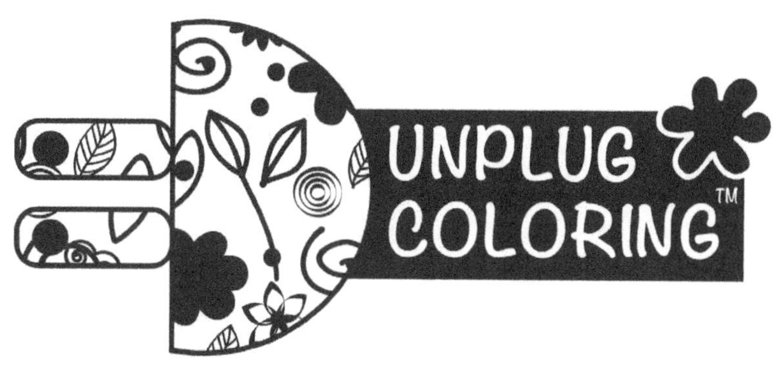

Companion Edition also available from Unplug Coloring!

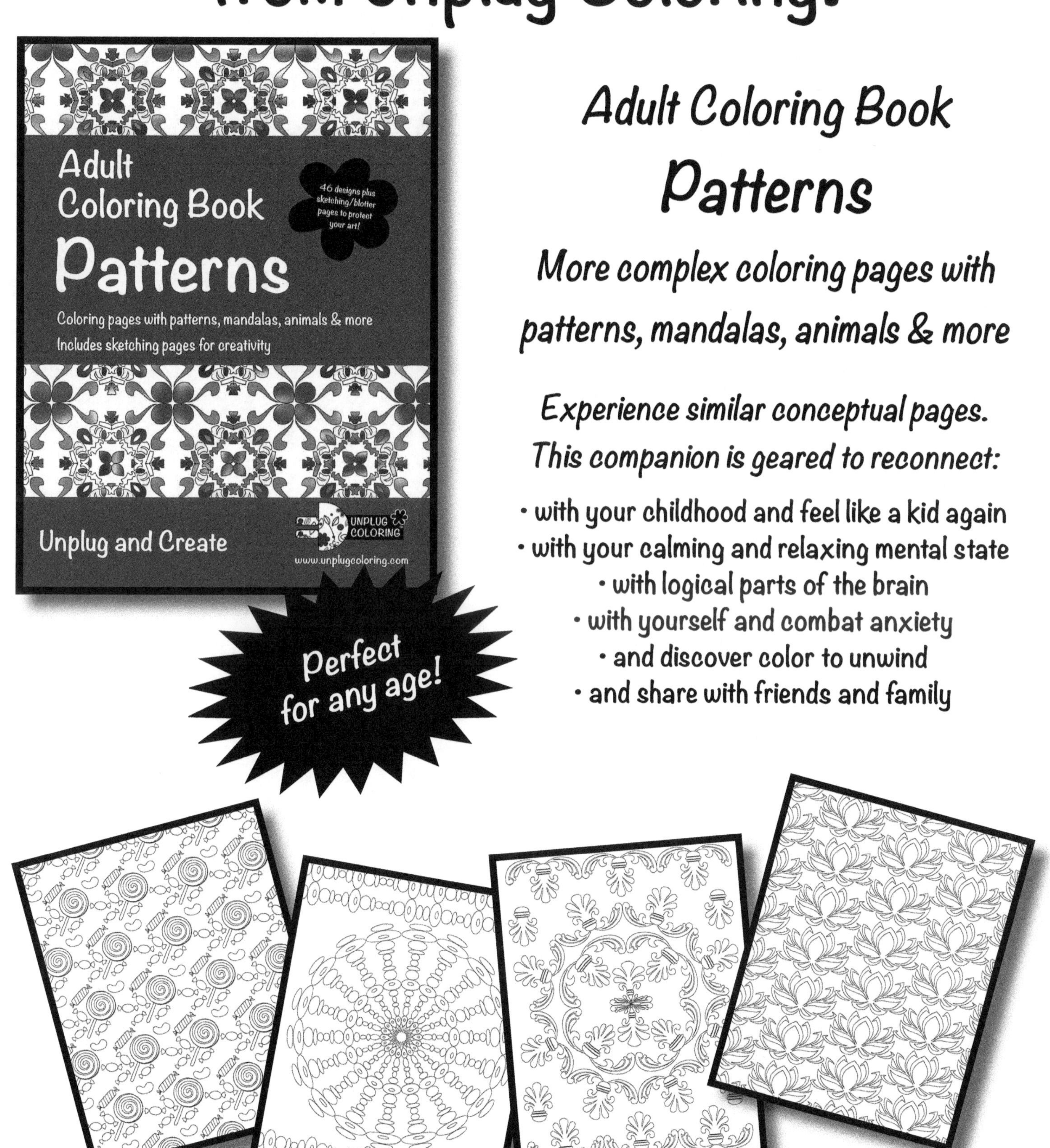

www.ingramcontent.com/pod-product-compliance
Lightning Source LLC
LaVergne TN
LVHW081402110826
845149LV00010B/1644
* 9 7 8 0 9 9 7 4 9 0 0 3 9 *